Macmillan/McGraw-Hill READING

Contributors

The Princeton Review, Time Magazine, Accelerated Reader

The Princeton Review is not
affiliated with Princeton
University or ETS.

Students with print disabilities may be eligible to obtain an accessible, audio version of the pupil edition of this textbook. Please call Recording for the Blind & Dyslexic at 1-800-221-4792 for complete information.

Macmillan/McGraw-Hill

A Division of The McGraw·Hill Companies

Published by Macmillan/McGraw-Hill, a division of The McGraw-Hill Companies, Inc., Two Penn Plaza, NY, NY 10121

Printed in the United States of America

ISBN 0-02-188569-9/3, Bk.2
2 3 4 5 6 7 8 9 058/043 04 03 02

Macmillan/McGraw-Hill READING

Authors

James Flood

Jan E. Hasbrouck

James V. Hoffman

Diane Lapp

Donna Lubcker

Angela Shelf Medearis

Scott Paris

Steven Stahl

Josefina Villamil Tinajero

Karen D. Wood

Macmillan
McGraw-Hill

New York   Farmington

UNIT 1

Tell Me More

4

UNIT 2

Think It Through

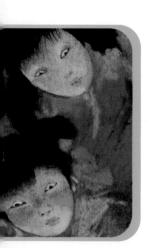

6

UNIT 3

Turning Points

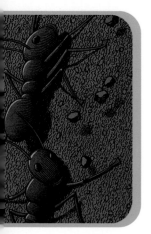

8

10

Tell Me More

Who Has Seen the Wind?

Who has seen the wind?
　　Neither I nor you.
But when the leaves hang trembling,
　　The wind is passing through.

Who has seen the wind?
　　Neither you nor I.
But when the trees bow down their heads,
　　The wind is passing by.

by Christina Rossetti

If you look at this painting quickly, you might just see some bushes, rocks, and snow. But if you look again, you will see that there are animals in it.

Look at the painting. What animal do you see? Is there more than one? Where do you think the footprints came from? Do you think the animal made those footprints recently? Explain your reasons.

Look at the painting again. Why does the animal blend into the bushes?

Doubled Back by Bev Doolittle, 1988

How Anansi

Develop a strategy for recognizing the order of events in a story.

1 **Find out what happens first** in the story. Then look for the events that happen after that.

2 **Look for time-order words** such as *later* and *then*. They are clue words that help you to know when events happen.

3 **Picture each event** that takes place in the story. Does each event lead to the next one?

4 **Retell the events** in your own words. What happens to Anansi in the story?

Anansi was a spider who loved to play tricks. One morning, as Anansi was crawling on the walls of the royal palace, he noticed the King sitting on his throne.

Very politely, Anansi greeted the King. "Good day," he said. "Did you know that I ride on Tiger's back each evening?"

The King held his belly and laughed. "Anansi, I doubt that very much!"

Later that day, the King called Tiger to his palace. "Anansi tells me that he rides on your back each evening. Is that true?" the King asked.

"Of course not!" Tiger bellowed. "In fact, I'll prove it to you!"

Then Tiger stomped to Anansi's home in the forest. "Anansi!" he called. "How dare you tell a lie to the King! Go back immediately and tell him it is not so!"

Tricked Tiger

Anansi said, "Okay, I will do as you command, but I have a stomach ache right now and it really hurts. Could you please give me a ride to the palace?"

Anxious to get this situation settled, Tiger agreed. So Anansi rode on his back to the palace.

"You see, King!" Anansi called out gleefully, as they approached the palace. "I did not lie to you. I *do* ride Tiger each evening!"

Tiger bellowed again, this time louder than ever. He had been tricked by Anansi, who just laughed and laughed and laughed.

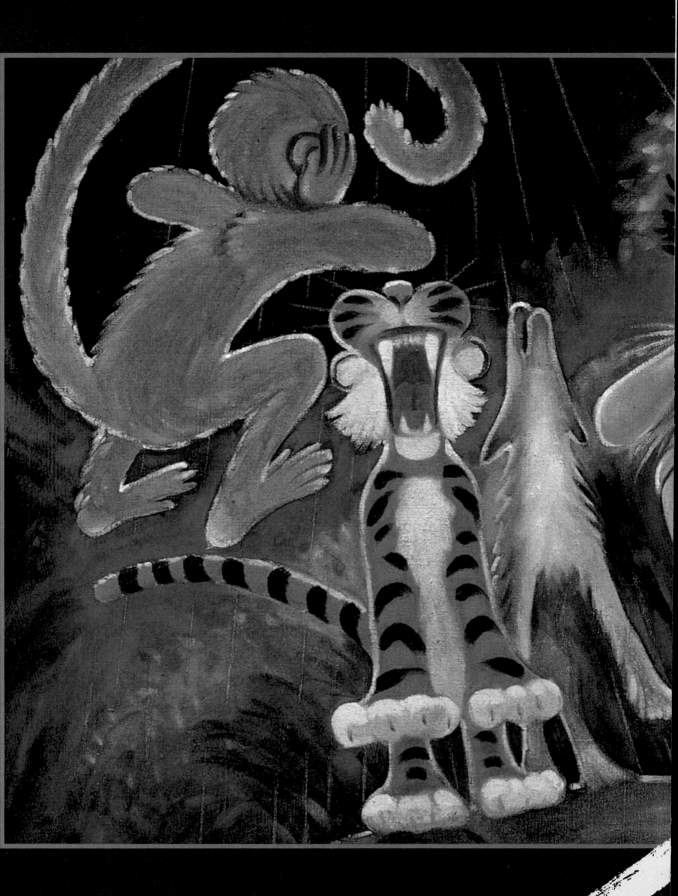

The Terrible EEK

A Japanese Tale

Retold by Patricia A. Compton

Illustrated by Sheila Hamanaka

A long time ago, in a certain place in the mountains, it began to rain. The wind shook a small house with a thatch roof.

Inside, a boy and his father sat warming their hands over a small fire. Nearby, the boy's mother prepared the evening meal.

The sounds of the wind and rain battering at the house frightened the little boy. "Father, are you ever afraid?" the boy asked.

"Yes, my son, there are things that I fear," the father answered.

"What do you fear most?" the boy asked.

"Among humans," the father replied, "I am most afraid of a thief."

It happened that a thief had climbed on to the thatch roof of the house and was hiding up there. When the thief heard the father's reply, he was triumphant. "I am the strongest and most fearsome of creatures," he said to himself. "I am what they are most afraid of."

"Among animals," the father continued, "I am most afraid of the wolf."

At that very moment, a wolf was sneaking by the side of the house with plans to steal a chicken or two for his dinner.

The wolf sniffed haughtily and said to himself, "I am the strongest and most fearsome of creatures. I am what they are most afraid of."

"But the most frightening thing of all to me," the father went on telling his son, "is a terrible leak. I hope there are no leaks tonight."

The wolf stopped a moment and thought, "What is a terrible leak?" He had never heard of a terrible leak. It must be an awful creature if they are most afraid of it.

A noisy gust of wind blew away some of the sounds of the father's words before they reached the thief on the roof. All he heard was ". . . the most frightening thing of all is a terrible eek."

The thief wondered what a terrible eek could be. He reached up to scratch his head and lost his balance. Then he slipped on the wet thatch and slid off the roof, landing right on the back of the wolf.

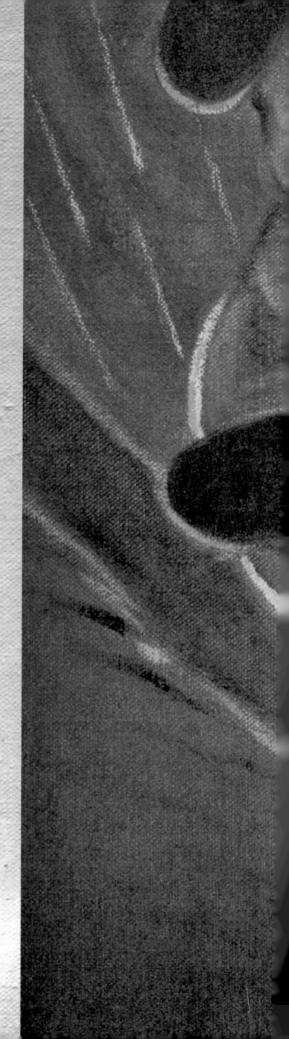

Now the poor thief thought he had landed on the back of the terrible eek. And the wolf thought that the terrible leak had landed on him.

The wolf howled, then ran with all his might toward the woods. He was hoping the terrible leak would fall off. The thief clutched the wolf's neck and hung on with all his might.

As they sped through the forest, the thief saw a low-hanging branch.

In one quick motion, he let go of the wolf's neck, grabbed the branch, and swung free.

The thief was so relieved to be away from the terrible eek that he did not notice that the branch was too weak to hold him. It cracked and he fell.

It happened that there was a deep hole right under the tree. The thief tumbled into the hole and could not climb up the steep, slippery sides.

The wolf, feeling the weight leave his back, ran to his den. Once there he collapsed, completely out of breath. After the wolf finally caught his breath, he felt very thirsty. He peered cautiously out of his den. Not seeing anything, he went to the water hole for a drink. There he met a tiger.

"Tiger, do you know what a terrible leak is?" asked the wolf. "Humans fear it more than anything. It jumped on my back and nearly choked me to death. Will you help me catch the leak?"

"I have never heard of a terrible leak. I thought I was the strongest and most frightening creature in the world," the tiger said. "Yes, I will go with you to catch the terrible leak."

A monkey sitting in a nearby tree heard the tiger and the wolf talking. "Where are you going?" he asked.

"We are going to catch the terrible leak," said the tiger. "Will you come along and help us?"

"I have never heard of a terrible leak, and I am not strong and frightening like you are," said the monkey, "but I am clever. So I will come and help you catch it."

The tiger and the monkey followed the wolf back to the tree where the terrible leak had jumped off the wolf's back.

The monkey found the big hole under the tree and said, "I will put my tail down into the hole and see if the leak tries to grab it."

"Are you there, terrible leak?" cried the monkey, lowering his tail into the hole.

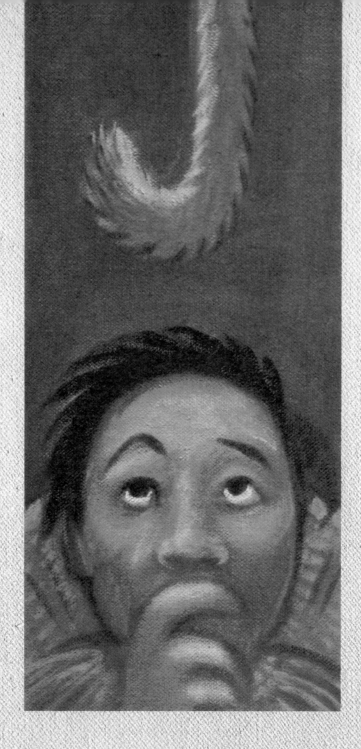

When the thief saw the
monkey's tail, he grabbed tight
and pulled.

The monkey became very
frightened, and he pulled with all
his might. The monkey pulled the
thief right out of the hole.

The tiger roared, the wolf howled, the monkey screeched, and the thief yelled.

This awful noise frightened them all so much that they ran off into the woods and never ever found out about the terrible leak.

After a while, the rain stopped and the moon came out and shone on the little house with the thatch roof.

The boy and his mother and father were sound asleep in their dry, warm beds.

Meet
Patricia A. Compton

Patricia Compton starts with an idea of a story she wants to tell. She likes to sketch, rather than write, her ideas. Compton says, "The words come after the pictures. Then the story changes over time as I get a feel for the characters and where they lead me."

Meet
Sheila Hamanaka

A third-generation Japanese American, Sheila Hamanaka is proud of her heritage. Much of her work is based on Japanese themes and art.

Hamanaka especially enjoys drawing people and animals. She says, "I always try to draw different types of people—all ages, colors, sizes, girls and boys—because we live in a multicultural world."

Story Questions & Activities

1 What does the wolf do when the thief lands on him?

2 How does the wolf get the tiger and monkey to go after the "leak"?

3 How might the thief describe the "terrible eek"?

4 What is this story mostly about?

5 Think about the wolves in this story and "Dream Wolf." How are they alike? different?

Write a Letter

Pretend you are one of the animals in "The Terrible Eek." Write a letter to another character explaining why you are the "most fearsome of creatures." To support your argument, compare yourself to the other characters.

Create an Uchiwa

The Japanese keep cool using paper fans called *uchiwa*.
Create one yourself. First, draw a pretty picture on paper.
Next, fold the paper back and forth. Each fold
should be about half an inch wide. Then,
staple the bottom end together.
Finally, tie a stick to the bottom
for you to hold.

Make Masks

In Japanese Noh plays, actors
wear masks that show how each
character feels. Make two Noh
masks. One should show a
character who is very scary. The
other should show a character who
is very frightened.

Find Out More

Are there really wolves,
tigers, and monkeys in Japan?
Think about where you might find
that information. Then find out.

Read a Chart

A **chart** shows information using headings, lists, and columns. This chart gives information about rainfall in Japan.

Average Yearly Rainfall in Japan

City	Inches	Centimeters
Hokkaido	33	84
Tokyo	62	158
Honshu	150	380

Use the chart to answer these questions.

1 How many columns does the chart have?

2 What information does the first column show?

3 How many centimeters of rain does Tokyo usually get each year?

4 In which city does it rain the least?

5 Why is it sometimes more useful to show information in a chart rather than writing it out in sentences?

TEST POWER

DIRECTIONS:

Read the story. Then read each question about the story.

SAMPLE

A Summer on the Ranch

Rachel spent a summer working at her uncle's horse ranch. She had always liked horses and looked forward to the summer for a long time.

Rachel spent her first week helping her uncle feed the horses, brush them, and take them for a run.

One day, Rachel's uncle said he would show her how to put shoes on the horses' hooves.

Rachel knew the shoes were made of iron and were shaped like the letter "U".

"Doesn't that hurt?" Rachel asked when her uncle nailed the horseshoe onto the horse's hoof.

"No. A horse has no feeling in its hooves. The shoes protect the hooves and keep them from breaking or splitting."

1 Which happened last in the story?

○ Rachel brushed the horses.

○ Rachel came to the ranch.

○ Rachel fed the horses.

○ Rachel's uncle put shoes on the horses.

2 Why did Rachel want to spend the summer at the ranch?

○ She liked horses.

○ She liked horseshoes.

○ She liked ranches.

○ She did not like school.

Stories in Art

When you look at this painting, you almost feel like you are sitting in the boat, too. That's because the artist painted it from a certain point of view.

Look at the painting. What part of the boat do you see? If you were taking a photo of this scene, where would you sit? What can you tell about the woman holding the baby?

Close your eyes. What do you remember about the painting? Why?

The Boating Party by Mary Cassatt, 1893–1894

National Gallery of Art, Washington, D.C.

Author's Purpose and Point of View

Develop a strategy for recognizing author's purpose and point of view.

1 **Why did the author** write the article? What or whom is the article about?

2 **Identify the author's purpose.** Does the author present facts about the subject?

3 **Look for clues** to the author's viewpoint. How does the author feel about the subject?

4 **Explain the author's purpose** and point of view. Does the author want others to learn about Diego Rivera? How can you tell?

Diego Rivera

Diego Rivera was born in Mexico in 1886. As an artist, he is best known for his murals. Murals are pictures that are painted directly on a wall. They are usually in public spaces. Rivera liked to paint murals because everyone could see and enjoy them. He painted murals in Mexico and in the United States.

Today, his paintings are treasures in both countries. But that hasn't always been true.

In 1932, Diego Rivera was asked to paint some murals for the Detroit Institute of Arts. Detroit was then the car-making capital of the world. Rivera spent months studying Detroit's factories. He made thousands of drawings. In the end, Rivera created four paintings about factories and working people.

Some people were unhappy with the murals and wanted them removed. The working people shown in the pictures came out by the thousands, during their time off, to make sure the murals would not be removed. Letters came in from museum directors and artists praising Rivera's work.

The people's voices were heard. This great art would stay. Today, the murals attract visitors from all over the world.

MEET
CARMEN LOMAS GARZA

Birthdays and fairs, tasty *empanadas,*
and *piñatas* packed with sweets—these
were all a part of the Mexican-American
community of Kingsville, Texas. This was
where Carmen Lomas Garza was born and
raised. Today, she keeps these memories
alive through her many works of art.

Lomas Garza was thirteen years old
when she decided to become an artist.
Today, she is considered one of the leading
Mexican-American painters. Her work
has been featured in museums all over
the world.

In My Family
En Mi Familia

"Baile en 1958"
©1995 CARMEN LOMAS GARZA

Pictures and Stories by
Carmen Lomas Garza

CARMEN LOMAS GARZA
©1995

THE HORNED TOADS

When we were kids, my mother and grandmother would get mad at us for playing in the hot sun in the middle of the day. They'd say we were just like the horned toads at high noon, playing outside without a care.

I was fascinated by the horned toads. They're shaped like frogs, but they're not frogs. They're lizards. They have horns all over their bodies to protect them from bigger animals that want to eat them.

Here's my brother Arturo, trying to feed an ant to a horned toad. I'm behind him, on my toes, because I don't want the ants to crawl up on me. Those are fire ants. They can really sting.

LOS CAMALEONES

Cuando éramos niños, mi mamá y mi abuela se enojaban con nosotros cuando jugábamos bajo el sol caliente del mediodía. Nos decían que éramos como los camaleones al mediodía que juegan sin importarles nada.

Yo estaba fascinada por los camaleones. Se parecen a las ranas, pero no son ranas. Son lagartijas. Tienen cuernos por todo el cuerpo para protegerse de animales más grandes que quieran comérselos.

Aquí está mi hermano Arturo dándole de comer una hormiga a un camaleón. Yo estoy atrás de él, de puntitas, pues no quiero que se me suban las hormigas. Ésas son hormigas coloradas. Son de las que sí pican.

CLEANING NOPALITOS

This is my grandfather, Antonio Lomas. He's shaving off the thorns from freshly cut cactus pads, called *nopalitos*. My sister Margie is watching him work.

Nopalitos are called "the food of last resort," because back when there were no refrigerators and your winter food supply would run out, you knew you could eat the cactus pads through the last days of winter and the early days of spring.

My grandmother would boil the *nopalitos* in salt water, cut them up, and stir-fry them with chile and eggs for breakfast.

LIMPIANDO NOPALITOS

Éste es mi abuelo, Antonio Lomas. Les está quitando las espinas a las pencas recién cortadas, llamadas nopalitos. Mi hermana Margie lo observa hacer esta labor.

Los nopalitos también son conocidos como "la comida del último recurso", pues cuando no había refrigeradores y se acababan las provisiones de comida de invierno, uno sabía que podía comerse las pencas del nopal hasta que terminara el invierno y llegaran los primeros días de la primavera.

Mi abuela hervía los nopalitos en agua con sal, los cortaba en cachitos, y los freía con chile y huevo para el desayuno.

EMPANADAS

Once every year my Aunt Paz and Uncle Beto would make dozens and dozens of *empanadas*, sweet turnovers filled with sweet potato or squash from their garden. They would invite all the relatives and friends to come over, and you could eat as many as you wanted. They lived in a little one-bedroom house, and every surface in the house was covered with a plate of *empanadas*. There was no place to sit down.

There's Uncle Beto, rolling out the dough. Aunt Paz, in the yellow dress with the red flowers, is spreading in the filling. My mother and father are drinking coffee. That's me in the blue dress.

EMPANADAS

Una vez al año mi tía Paz y mi tío Beto hacían docenas y docenas de empanadas, dulces panecillos rellenos de camote o calabaza de su jardín. Invitaban a todos los parientes y amigos a que vinieran a probarlas y uno se podía comer todas las que quisiera. Mis tíos vivían en una casita de un cuarto y todas las superficies disponibles en la casa se cubrían con platos llenos de empanadas. No había lugar donde sentarse.

Allí está mi tío Beto extendiendo con un rodillo la masa. Mi tía Paz, que lleva un vestido amarillo con flores rojas, les pone el relleno. Mi mamá y mi papá toman café. La del vestido azul soy yo.

BIRTHDAY BARBECUE

This is my sister Mary Jane's birthday party. She's hitting a piñata that my mother made. My mother also baked and decorated the cake. There she is, bringing the meat that's ready to cook. My father is cooking at the barbecue, which he designed and built himself. My grandfather is shoveling in the coals of mesquite wood.

Underneath the tree are some young teenagers, very much in love. My great uncle is comforting my young cousin, who was crying, and encouraging him to hit the piñata. My grandmother is holding a baby. She was always holding the babies, and feeding them, and putting them to sleep.

BARBACOA PARA CUMPLEAÑOS

Ésta es la fiesta de cumpleaños de mi hermana Mary Jane. Ella le pega a la piñata que le hizo mi mamá. Mi mamá también hizo y decoró el pastel. Allí está ella trayendo la carne lista para cocinarse. Mi papá cocina en el horno de barbacoa que diseñó y construyó él mismo. Mi abuelo está con una pala echándole carbón de leña de mezquite.

Bajo el árbol están unos jovencitos muy enamorados. Mi tío consuela a mi primito que llora, y lo anima a que le pegue a la piñata. Mi abuela lleva en brazos a un bebé. Ella siempre llevaba en brazos a bebés, les daba de comer y los ponía a dormir.

"Baile en 1958"
©1995 CARMEN LOMAS GARZA

DANCE AT EL JARDÍN

This is a Saturday night at *El Jardín*, a neighborhood restaurant in my home town. It's the summer, so warm that you can dance outside. A *conjunto* band is playing—drums, accordion, guitar, and bass. This is the music I grew up with. Everybody's dancing in a big circle: the young couples, the older couples, and the old folks dancing with the teenagers or children. Even babies get to dance.

I learned to dance from my father and grandfather. This is where my love of dance started. To me, dance means *fiesta*, celebration. You have the music, the beautiful clothes, and all the family members dancing together. It's like heaven. It is heaven.

BAILE EN EL JARDÍN

Ésta es una noche de sábado en *El Jardín*, un restaurante familiar de mi pueblo natal. Es verano y hace tanto calor que la gente baila afuera. Un conjunto toca con tambora, acordeón, guitarra y bajo. Ésta es la música con la que crecí. Todos bailan formando un gran círculo: las parejas jóvenes, las parejas más grandes, y los viejitos bailan con adolescentes o criaturas. Hasta los bebés se ponen a bailar.

Yo aprendí a bailar con mi padre y mi abuelo. De ahí nació mi amor por el baile. Para mí, el baile representa fiesta, celebración. Aquí está la música, los hermosos vestidos, y todos los miembros de la familia bailan juntos. Es como el cielo. Es la gloria.

Story Questions & Activities

1. How did the author feel about horned toads?

2. Why are *nopalitos* called "the food of last resort"?

3. Do you think that the author enjoyed her childhood? Explain.

4. What is the main idea of this selection?

5. Compare one painting from "In My Family" with the painting on page 38. How are they alike and different?

Write an Essay

Write an essay comparing and contrasting what is going on in the empanada picture (page 46) and the birthday barbecue picture (page 49). Be sure to give specific details.

Create a Breakfast Menu

Sometimes the author's family ate *nopalitos* with chile and eggs for breakfast. What do you like to eat in the morning? Create a breakfast menu for a restaurant. Write down what people can order to eat and drink. Include prices and maybe even some drawings.

Celebrate Your Community

In this selection, Carmen Lomas Garza celebrates her family and community. What would you like people to know about your family or community? Plan a short presentation to celebrate the people and places around you.

Find Out More

This selection details some fascinating traditions of Mexicans and Mexican Americans. But there's much more to learn! Choose one topic to learn about, such as games or holidays and celebrations. Share what you learn with the class.

Use a Diagram

A family tree is a diagram that shows how family members are related. Elena Serna made this family tree. It gives the names of her parents, grandparents, and great-grandparents.

Use the family tree to answer these questions.

1 How many of Elena's grandparents does the family tree show?

2 What are the names of Elena's parents?

3 What is the name of Elena's grandmother on her father's side of the family?

4 What is the name of Manolo Tinao's father?

5 Which relative was Elena probably named after?

TEST POWER

Test Tip

Reading the story slowly and carefully will make it easier to answer the questions.

DIRECTIONS:

Read the story. Then read each question about the story.

SAMPLE

Trip to the Bakery

Mr. Keenan opened the door to the bakery. Jessica and the class rushed inside. Everyone smelled the delicious cookies baking. The baker wore a tall white cap. He told the children, "Every morning I get up at four o'clock to bake dozens of cookies." He gave everyone a cookie and said, "Let me tell you my secret to making the best cookies."

Jessica said, "No one makes cookies better than my mom does."

The baker heard her and asked, "Does your mother use almonds in her cookies?"

"That's exactly what she uses in her cookies!" Jessica said. "How did you know?"

The baker smiled and said, "That is the secret of a very good baker!"

1 What happened first?

○ The baker told his secret.

○ Mr. Keenan opened the door.

○ Jessica smiled.

○ The baker talked to the group.

2 How does Jessica feel at the end of the story?

○ Tired

○ Sad

○ Angry

○ Proud

Why are your answers correct?

55

Stories in Art

Photographs can help us to see things in a new way. A landscape can look completely different through the lens of a camera.

What do you think this is a photograph of? What do you think happened to make the cracks in the ground? How would this landscape look different after a rainstorm?

Look at the photograph again. What does it make you think of? Why?

**Mesquite Flat Dunes,
Death Valley
National Park
by Carl Clifton**

A Tiny

Cause and Effect

Develop a strategy to identify cause and effect.

① **Identify the subject** of the article. What is the article about?

② **Find details that** tell you why something happened. This is the *cause.*

③ **Look for details** that tell you what happened. This is the effect.

④ **Look for clue words,** such as *because, if,* and *in order to*. These words signal cause-effect relationships.

⑤ **State a cause and its effect.** Why does the elf owl only hunt at night?

Elf owls are one of many creatures that live in the desert. These tiny birds live in Arizona, California, New Mexico, and Texas. They spend the winter in southern Mexico and Central America.

Elf owls are the smallest owls in North America. About the size of a sparrow, they are only six inches long, with very short tails. Their wingspan is about 15 inches.

Elf owls are either gray or brown. They have a white breast, and white feathers above their eyes that look like eyebrows. Their eyes are yellow.

They feed on insects, centipedes, scorpions, lizards and mice. Because elf owls are nocturnal, they hunt for food at night. If an elf owl senses danger, it will often play dead in order to fool its enemies.

Desert Bird

Elf owls nest in the holes in old cacti, dead trees, and even fence posts. As more people move into the desert and build homes, the elf owls have fewer places to nest. Ecologists are studying elf owl habits. They hope that the owl can learn to use nest boxes. If this attempt to save the elf owl is successful, this tiny bird may yet be able to survive in America.

Meet
Brenda Z. Guiberson

Brenda Guiberson got the idea for Cactus Hotel after several trips with her family to the Arizona desert. The sights and sounds of the desert thrilled her.

Guiberson enjoys researching and writing children's books. She says, "It's hard work but fun and surprises pop up all along the way."

Meet
Megan Lloyd

For Megan Lloyd, research is a very big part of her work. When she draws pictures for fiction stories, Lloyd uses costumes and lighting to explore the characters and setting. She says, "With nonfiction books, I carry my research even further, usually traveling to the geographical location in which the book is set."

Lloyd's research has taken her from the Saguaro National Monument in Tucson, Arizona (for Cactus Hotel) to a lobster boat off the coast of Maine!

CACTUS HOTEL

Written by Brenda Z. Guiberson

Illustrated by Megan Lloyd

On a hot, dry day in the desert, a bright-red fruit falls from a tall saguaro cactus. *Plop*. It splits apart on the sandy floor. Two thousand black seeds glisten in the sunlight.

When the air cools in the evening, an old pack rat comes out and eats the juicy fruit. Then he skitters across the sand. A seed left clinging to his whiskers falls off under a paloverde tree.

It is a good place for the seed to drop. A spotted ground squirrel looking for something to eat does not see it. A house finch chirping high in the paloverde does not see it.

After many dry days, a heavy rain falls on the desert.
Soon a young cactus sprouts up from the ground.

Slowly, slowly the seedling grows. The paloverde
protects it from the hot summer sun and cold winter
nights. After ten years the cactus is only four inches high.
It is just big enough for desert ants to climb its spiny
sides.

After a rainstorm, when the desert blooms with color, the cactus pulls in water with its long roots and looks fat. A young pack rat stops to drink the water that drips off the tree. Then she scurries off, looking for a dry place to make a nest.

When there is no rain, the cactus uses up the water it has stored inside and looks thin. The paloverde loses its tiny leaves. But there is always some shade for the cactus below. After twenty-five years, the cactus is two feet tall. A jackrabbit cools off beside it and gnaws on the green pulp. But when a coyote moves in the distance, the jackrabbit disappears into a nearby hole.

After fifty years the cactus stands ten feet tall and
looks straight and strong beside the old paloverde. For the
very first time, brilliant white-and-yellow flowers appear
at the top of the cactus. Every spring from now on, the
flowers will open for one night only and then close in the
heat of the day. They beckon like a welcoming signal
across the desert. At different times of the day and night
birds, bees, and bats come for the nectar.

The flowers dry up, and after a month the bright-red fruit filled with black seeds is ripe and ready. A Gila woodpecker comes to eat. He looks around the cactus and decides to stay.

He has found the perfect place in the desert to begin a new hotel.

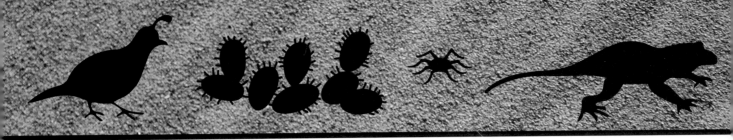

The woodpecker goes right to work, and the only tool he uses is his long, hard beak. *Tap, tap, tap.* He bores into the flesh of the cactus. *Tap, tap, tap.* He digs deep inside, to make a space that is comfortable and roomy.

The cactus is not harmed. It forms a tough scab all around the hole to protect itself from drying out. The woodpecker gets a weatherproof nest that is shady on hot days, and warm and insulated on frosty nights. And the cactus gets something in return: The woodpecker likes to eat the insects that can bring disease to the cactus.

After sixty years the cactus hotel is eighteen feet tall. To add more space, it begins to grow an arm. A woodpecker has a new hole in the trunk. Farther up, a white-winged dove makes a nest on the arm. And down below, an old hole is discovered by an elf owl. The birds feel safe, living high up in a prickly plant where nothing can reach them.

All around the desert there are holes of every size, for
ants and mice, lizards and snakes, rabbits and foxes. After
a hundred and fifty years, there are holes of every size
in the cactus, too. The giant plant has finally stopped
growing. It is fifty feet tall, with seven long branches.
It weighs eight tons—about as much as five automobiles.

Everybody wants to live in
the cactus hotel. Birds lay eggs
and pack rats raise their young.
Even insects and bats live there.

When one animal moves out,
another moves in. And every spring
they come for a special treat of nectar
and juicy red fruit.

73

Finally, after two hundred years, the old cactus sways
in a gust of wind and falls with a thud to the sandy floor.
Its great thorny arms crumble in the crash.

74

The creatures that lived up high must find other homes. But those that prefer to live down low move right in. A millipede, a scorpion, and many ants and termites quickly find homes in the toppled hotel.

After many months, all that remains are the wooden
ribs that supported the cactus while it stood so tall. A
collared lizard dashes over the top, looking for insects.
A ground snake huddles in the shade below.

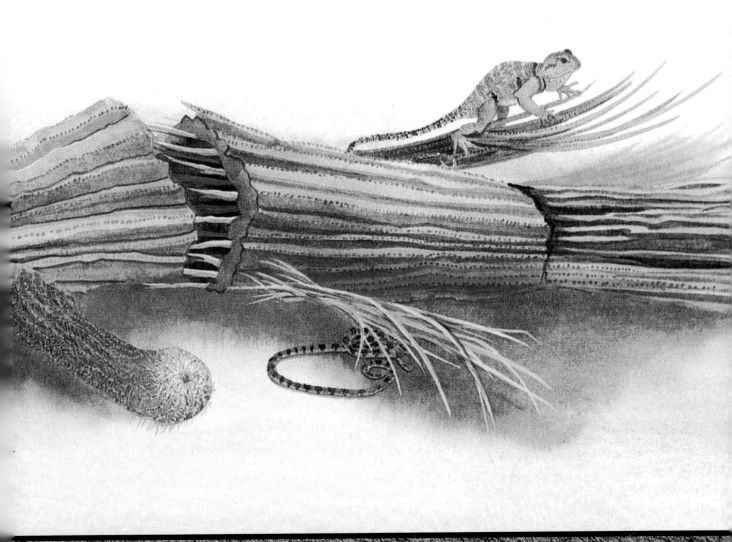

And all around, there is a forest of cacti slowly, slowly growing in the desert. Through hot and cold, wet and dry, some will survive long enough to become other cactus hotels.

Story Questions & Activities

1. How does the woodpecker help the cactus?

2. How does a rainstorm change the way a young cactus looks?

3. How is the saguaro cactus in the selection like a hotel?

4. What is the main idea of this selection?

5. "The Little Painter of Sabana Grande" tells about a community in Panama. In what ways does "Cactus Hotel" also tell about a community?

Write a Report

Different animals make use of the saguaro cactus in different ways. Write a report comparing and contrasting those ways. Be sure to support your comparisons with details.

80

Create a Poster

Look up "deserts" in an encyclopedia. Choose one to learn about. Gather facts such as average temperatures and amounts of rainfall. Also find out what plants and animals live there. Use what you learn to create a poster about the desert. Add illustrations.

Desert Silhouettes

Look at the art along the top and bottom of the pages of this selection. You will find silhouettes, or black outline drawings, of desert plants and creatures. Make your own desert silhouettes. First, cut plant or animal shapes out of black construction paper. Then glue the shapes onto color poster board.

Find Out More

Choose a tree or plant in your neighborhood. How many different creatures can you find there? With an adult, visit at different times of day and take notes. Draw a picture showing what you find.

Use a Chart

Charts may contain many kinds of information. Here is a chart that gives information about three kinds of cactus that grow in the southwestern region of the United States.

Kinds of Cactus Found in the Southwest

Cactus	Characteristics	Where Found	How Used
jumping cholla	• black trunk • spine-covered branches • average height: 4 to 6 feet	New Mexico	• stems fed to cattle
saguaro cactus	• woody ribs • average height: 50 feet	Arizona	• stems used for building materials
barrel cactus	• grows in clumps • red and yellow flowers • average height: $6\frac{1}{2}$ feet	Arizona	• source of fresh water in desert

Use the chart to answer these questions.

1 What information can you find in the first column?

2 What type of cactus does the second row tell about?

3 How is the barrel cactus used?

4 How tall does the jumping cholla usually grow?

5 Which cactus sounds the most interesting to you? Explain.

82

TEST POWER

Test Tip
If you do not understand a question, read it again carefully.

DIRECTIONS:

Read the story. Then read each question about the story.

SAMPLE

Mitch and the Paper Route

Mitch got a new bicycle with a basket big enough to carry newspapers. Mitch's brother Bob was going to summer camp for a week. Mitch was going to use his new bike to deliver Bob's papers for him while he was away. If he liked the job, Mitch might even try to get his own paper route.

On Saturday, the first day of the paper route, Mitch fell off his bike. Three newspapers were ruined when they fell in the mud. On Tuesday, he noticed he was delivering old newspapers from Monday and he had to start over. On Thursday, he was chased by a very big dog.

When Bob came home from camp he paid Mitch for his hard work and thanked him.

"Mitch, I've been invited to spend next week camping with the Wilsons. Will you do my paper route again?" Bob asked.

1 Mitch will probably try to —
   ○ give the money back to Bob
   ○ look for a different job
   ○ get a new bicycle
   ○ go for a bike ride

2 Which of these happened last?
   ○ Mitch was chased by a dog.
   ○ Bob paid Mitch.
   ○ Bob went to summer camp.
   ○ Mitch got a new bike.

Stories in Art

This painting is full of motion. Look at how the artist uses curves and lines to make the waves. These help to give the feeling of an ocean that is constantly moving.

Look at the painting. What can you tell about it? What are the whales doing? How do you think the artist feels about whales? Explain your reasons.

What colors did the artist use? What other details do you notice about the painting?

Celebration of the Whale by Liz Wright

84

Whales

Form Generalizations

Develop a strategy for forming generalizations.

1 **Read the title and the chart.** What is the article about?

2 **Look for clue words.** Words such as *most, some,* and *almost all* will help you recognize generalizations.

3 **Find sentences** in the article that contain clue words. Are any of them generalizations?

4 **Does the information** in the chart help you form generalizations?

5 **Generalize** about whales. Do the facts in the article support your generalization?

There are many kinds of whales. They can be put into two major groups: baleen whales and toothed whales. The humpback whale, the fin whale, the gray whale, and the huge blue whale are baleen whales. Baleen whales do not have teeth. Instead, they have hundreds of baleen plates, that hang down from the top of their mouths. The plates are made of whalebone and can be two to seven feet long. Baleen whales eat tiny sea animals called *krill.* They use the plates in their mouths to remove the krill from the water.

Pilot whales, beaked whales, killer whales, and sperm whales are toothed whales. They use their teeth to catch and eat fish and squid.

Most whales live in groups called pods, which travel and feed together. Some pods stay together for years.

Almost all whales make sounds. Scientists think whales use the sounds to talk to the rest of the pod. Most toothed whales make noises that sound like whistles or clicks. Some baleen whales click, too, while other baleen whales make low groans. The humpback whale repeats many kinds of sounds over and over in a kind of song.

As much as we know about these animals of the deep, there are still many secrets we have yet to learn about them.

Whales		
KIND OF WHALE	baleen whales	toothed whales
WHAT THEY EAT	krill	fish and squid
WHAT HELPS THEM EAT	baleen plates	teeth

Meet Nicola Davies

Nicola Davies lives in England. She has a college degree in zoology, the study of animals. Davies considers herself lucky to have had the opportunity to study blue whales, humpback whales, and sperm whales in the open ocean.

Blue whales are not always easy to find. Davies explains, "Unlike humpback whales, their booming hums are infrequent, so it is always exciting when we find one."

Meet Nick Maland

Nick Maland was sure he wanted to be an actor. Then one day Maland was asked to design the scenery and posters for a play. He discovered that he preferred art to acting and began a career as an illustrator. Maland spent 12 years illustrating books for adults before becoming a children's book illustrator.

BIG BLUE
WHALE

Written by **Nicola Davies**
Illustrated by **Nick Maland**

The blue whale is big.

Bigger than a giraffe.

Bigger than an elephant.

Bigger than a dinosaur.

The blue whale is
the biggest creature
that has ever lived
on Earth!

Female blue whales are
a little bigger than the males.

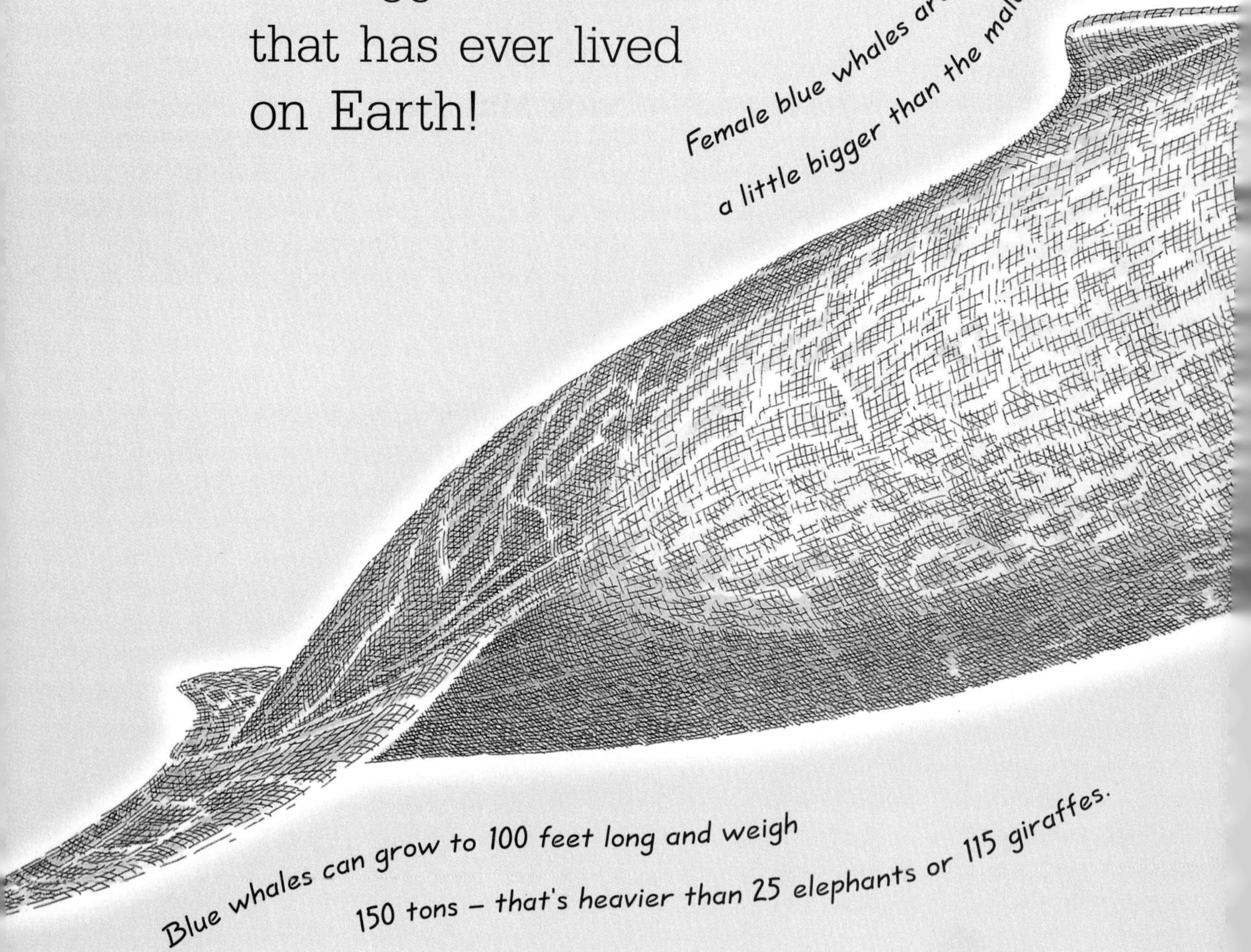

Blue whales can grow to 100 feet long and weigh
150 tons — that's heavier than 25 elephants or 115 giraffes.

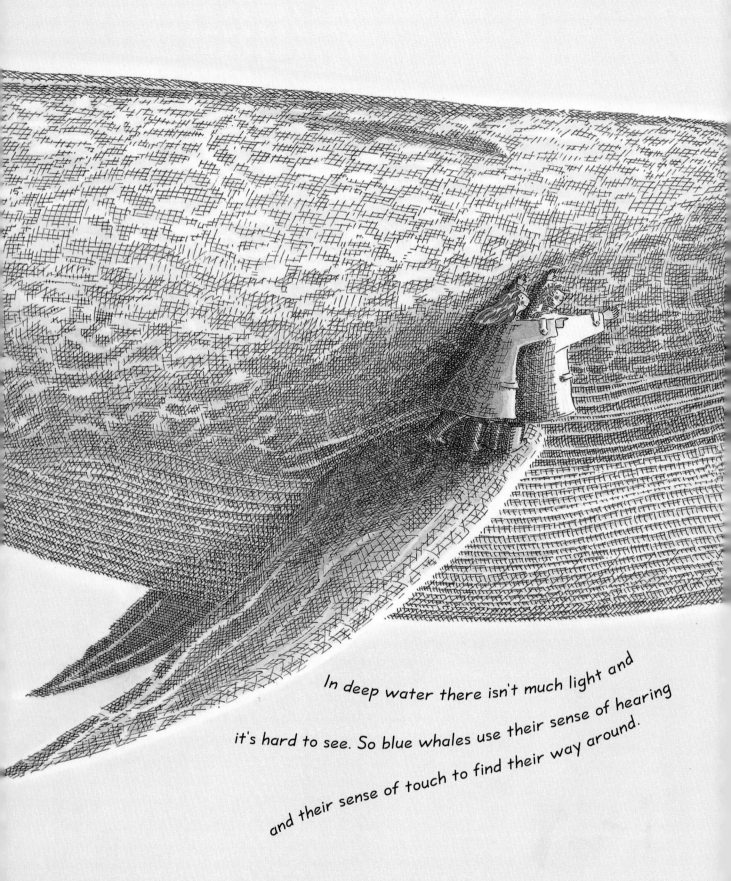

In deep water there isn't much light and it's hard to see. So blue whales use their sense of hearing and their sense of touch to find their way around.

Reach out and touch the blue whale's skin.
It's springy and smooth like a hard-
boiled egg, and it's as slippery
as wet soap.

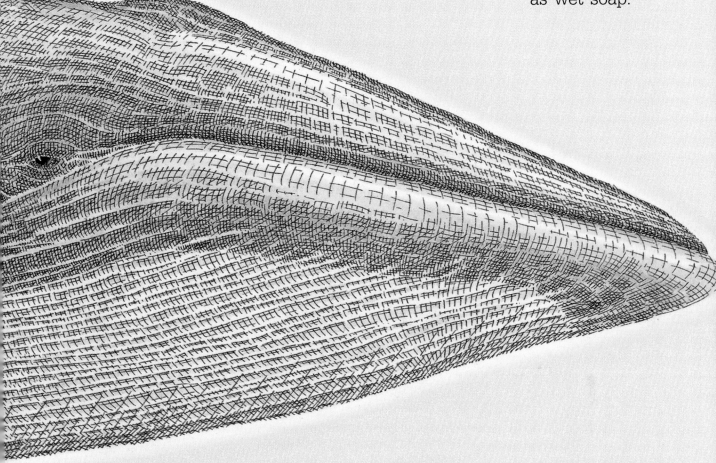

Look into its eye.
It's as big as a teacup and as dark
as the deep sea. Just behind the eye is a hole
as small as the end of a pencil. The hole is one of
the blue whale's ears—sticking-out ears would
get in the way when the whale is swimming.

The blue whale lives all of its long life in the sea.
But it is a mammal like us, and it breathes air, not water.

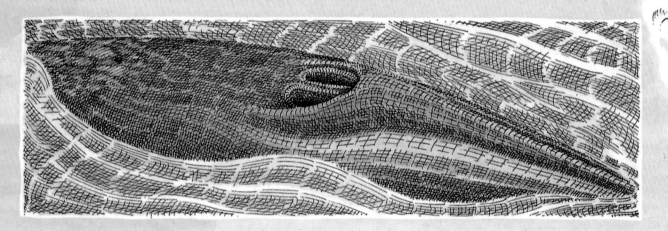

From time to time, it has to come to the surface to
breathe through the blowholes on top of its head.

Blue whales can live for about 70 to 80 years.

When it breathes out,
it makes a great misty puff
as high as a house.
This is the whale's blow,
and you can see it from far away.
You can hear it, too—a great

prOOUFF.

And if you are close enough,
you can smell it, as the whale's
breath is stale and fishy!

A blue whale can stay underwater for 30 minutes or more.
But on long journeys, it usually surfaces for air every 2 to 5 minutes.

A blue whale can have
as many as 790 baleen plates in its mouth.
Baleen is tough bendy stuff, like extra-hard fingernails.

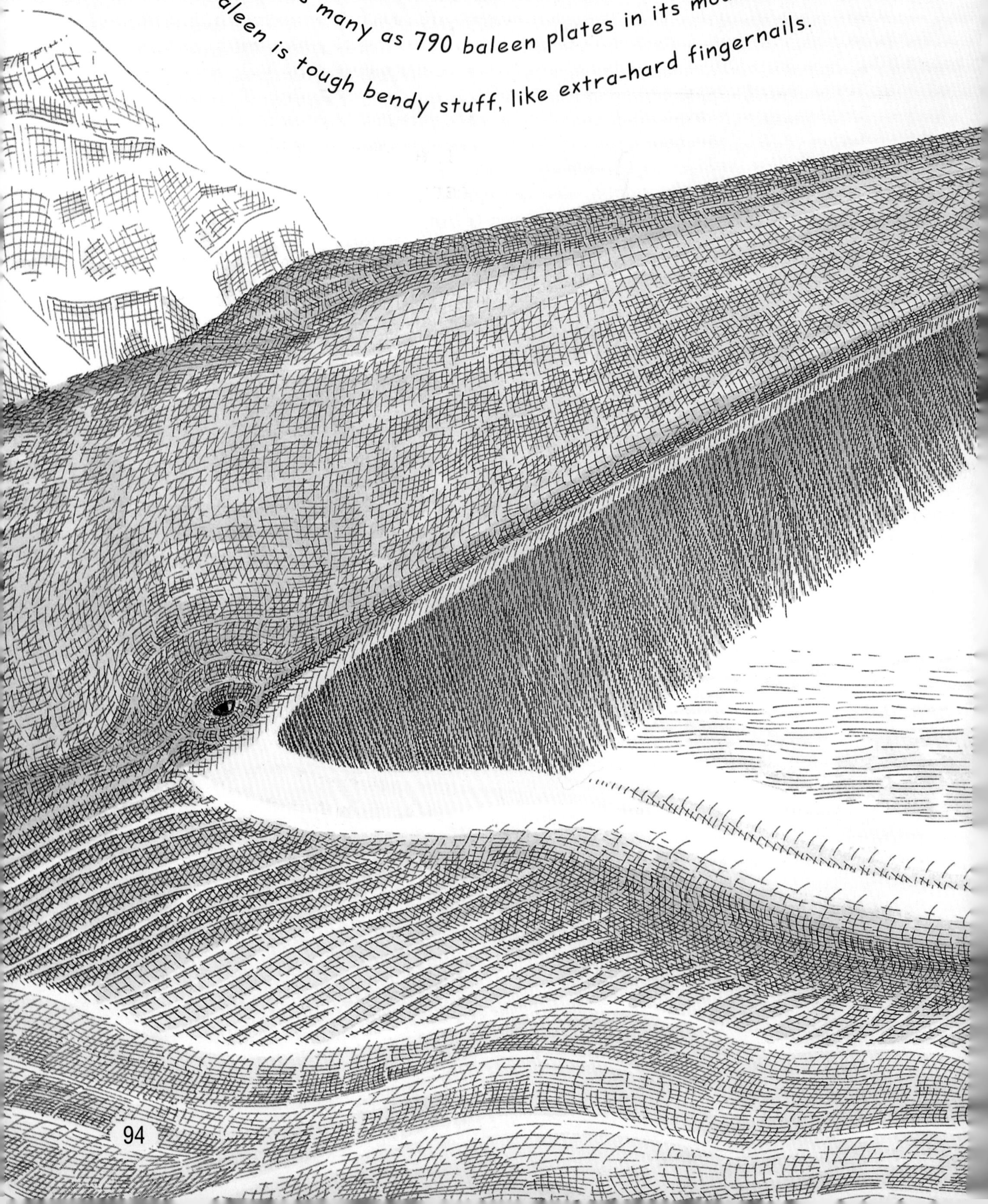

Take a look inside its mouth. Don't worry,
the blue whale doesn't eat people.
It doesn't even have any teeth. It has
hundreds of baleen plates, instead.
They're the long bristly things
hanging down from its top jaw.

The whale doesn't need teeth for biting
or chewing, because its food is tiny!

The blue whale eats krill—pale
pinkish shrimplike creatures the size of
your little finger.

Billions of them live in the cold seas around the North and South Poles. In summer there can be so many that the water looks pink—so that's when blue whales come to the polar seas to eat.

It takes an awful lot of tiny krill to feed a great big blue whale. But the whale doesn't catch them one at a time. It has a special way of swallowing whole swarms of them at once.

First, it takes a huge gulp of krill and salty seawater. There's room for all this because the whale's throat unfolds and opens out like a vast balloon.

Then it uses its big tongue to push the water out between its bristly baleen plates. The water streams away and leaves the krill caught on the bristles like peas in a sieve. Now all the whale has to do is lick them off and swallow them.

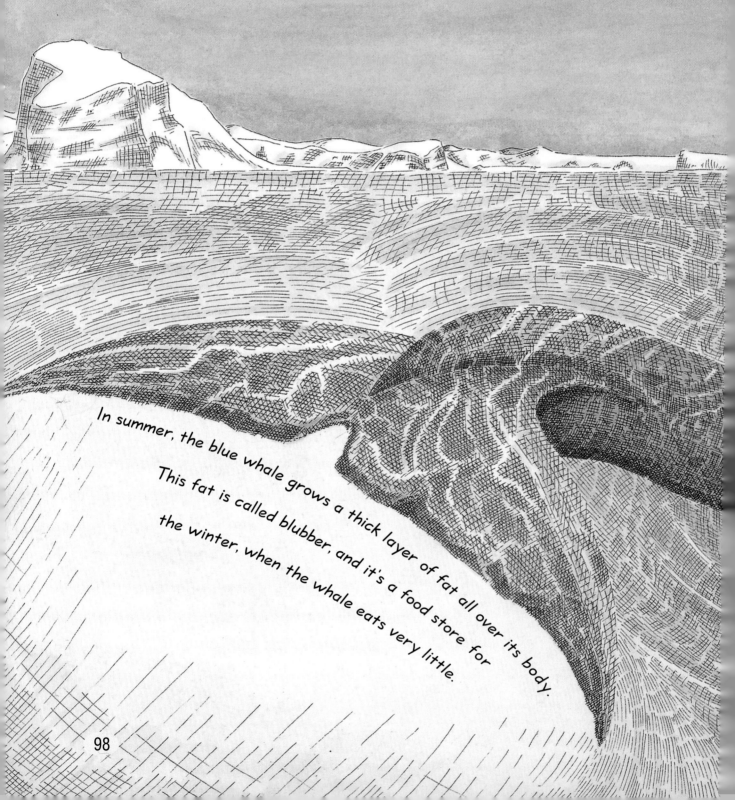

In summer, the blue whale grows a thick layer of fat all over its body. This fat is called blubber, and it's a food store for the winter, when the whale eats very little.

And this is how the blue whale spends the summer—eating krill and getting fat. But in the fall, the polar seas freeze over. The krill hide under the ice where the whale cannot catch them. So the whale swims away from the icy cold and the winter storms.

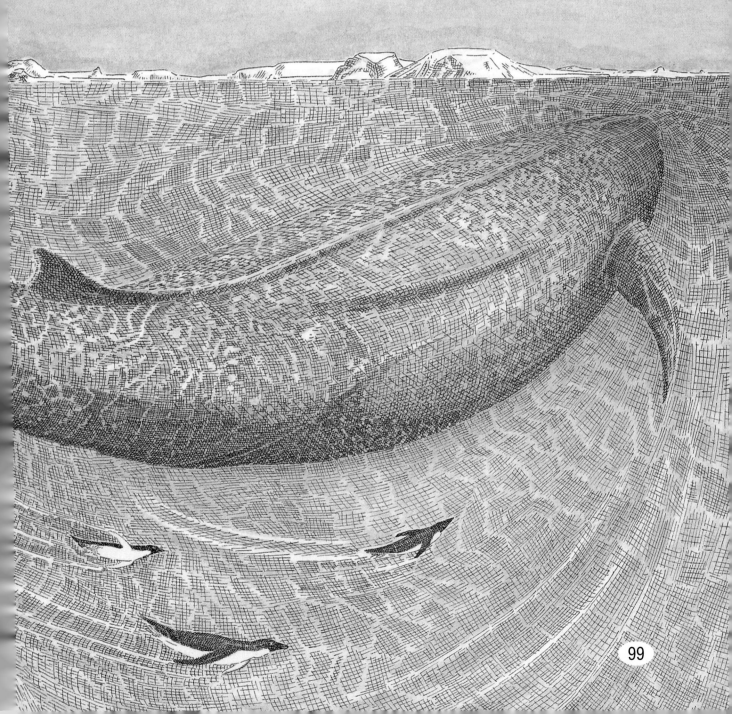

Day after day, the blue whale swims slowly and steadily toward its winter home. Its huge tail beats up and down to push it along. Its flippers steer it left or right.

For two months and more the whale swims, until at last it reaches the calm warm seas near the equator.

There it stays all winter.

Some blue whales spend their summers around the South Pole and swim north to the equator for the winter.

Others live around the North Pole and swim south for the winter.

But when it's winter at the South Pole, it's summer at the North Pole.

So the two groups of whales never meet.

And there the blue whale mother gives birth to her baby, where storms and cold weather can't hurt it.

The blue whale's baby slithers from her body, tail first. Gently she nudges it to the surface to take its first breath. Then the baby dives beneath her to take its first drink of milk.

Male and female blue whales mate in winter and then part. Babies are born about a year later.

All through the winter, the blue whale keeps her baby close. It feeds on her creamy milk, and it grows and grows.

In spring, the two whales return to the polar seas to feast on krill together. But by the fall, the young whale is big enough to live on its own.

So mother and young whale part and begin the long journey back to the equator.

A blue whale baby is 23 feet long at birth. It drinks more than 150 gallons of milk a day.

Adult blue whales make their hums in deep water. It's much colder than near the surface, which helps the hum to travel a long way.

A blue whale may travel from the polar seas to the equator and back every year of its life. Sometimes it will swim with other blue whales, but mostly it will swim alone.

Yet, the blue whale may not be as lonely as it seems. Because sometimes it makes a hum—a hum so loud and so low that it can travel for thousands of miles through the seas to reach other blue whales. Only a very low hum could travel so far. And only a very big animal could make a hum so low.

Perhaps that's why blue whales are the biggest creatures on Earth—so that they can talk to one another even when they are far apart. Who knows what they say. "Here I am!" would be enough ...

105

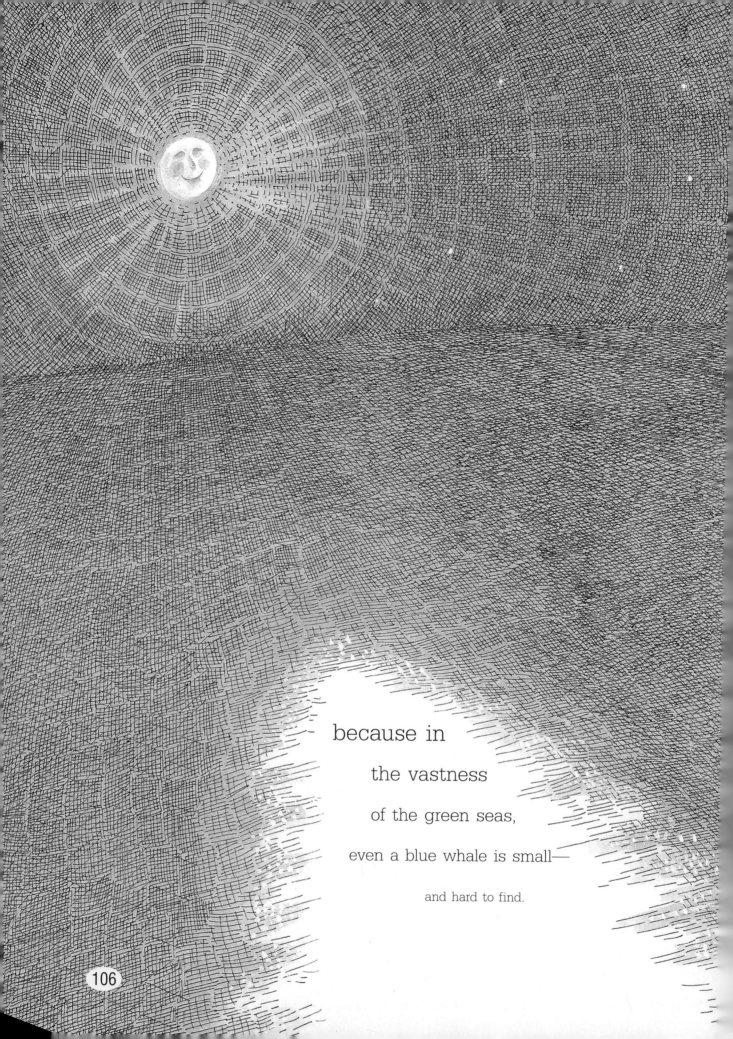

because in

the vastness

of the green seas,

even a blue whale is small—

and hard to find.

Story Questions & Activities

1. How do blue whales find their way around in deep water?

2. How does the blue whale feed?

3. Do you think the blue whale is a lonely animal? Why or why not?

4. What is the main idea of this selection?

5. Look back at the illustrations in "Big Blue Whale" and "Cactus Hotel." Do you like the fact that both stories used drawings instead of photographs? Why or why not?

Write a Story

Write a story about a mother blue whale and her baby. Include details that show their differences and similarities.

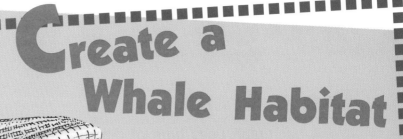

Create a Whale Habitat

Using the inside of a shoe box, design a habitat for a blue whale. Cut out pictures of the ocean from magazines. Make or draw different things you would see there. (Don't forget to include a big blue whale!)

Whale Baby Album

Create a "baby book" showing important events in a young whale's life. Include facts from this selection. Illustrate your album with drawings.

Find Out More

Blue whales are in danger of becoming extinct. Find out about another endangered animal, such as the bald eagle or red wolf. Also find out what people can do to help protect the animal.

Use a Graph

A bar graph uses bars of different lengths to show amounts. This bar graph shows the length of five types of whales.

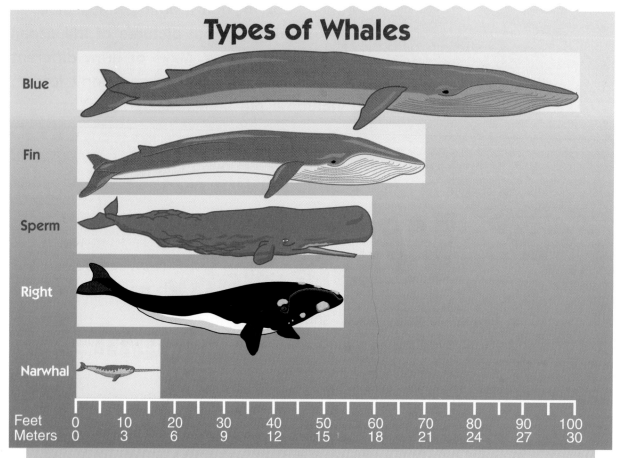

Types of Whales

	Feet	Meters
	0	0
	10	3
	20	6
	30	9
	40	12
	50	15
	60	18
	70	21
	80	24
	90	27
	100	30

Use the graph to answer these questions.

1. How many meters long is the fin whale?

2. Which whale on the graph is the shortest?

3. How many feet is the longest whale on the graph?

4. How many feet shorter is the right whale than the sperm whale?

5. Would a bar graph be a good way to show how many years different types of whales live? Explain.

110

TEST POWER

Test Tip

Remember, there is only one choice that answers the question best.

DIRECTIONS:

Read the story. Then read each question about the story.

SAMPLE

First Flight

May 17

My first airplane flight! Dad, Martha, and I arrived at the airport an hour before our plane was ready to leave. We answered questions about our luggage and watched our bags go on a big cart. Before we could go upstairs, we went through a "metal detector." It was interesting to see all of the machines that they use at the airport. My favorite thing so far was take-off.

June 2

I have been too busy to write! When we landed in Orlando, the plane really bumped. Everything else has been great. Now we are on the plane going home. When the plane took off, it seemed to go up even faster than before. Here comes our lunch now!

1 Which of these happened first on June 2?

○ Getting some lunch

○ Packing our bags

○ Answering some questions

○ The plane took off

2 Where is this diary being written?

○ In the airport

○ At Grandpa's house

○ In Orlando, Florida

○ On airplanes

111

Stories in Art

Some paintings focus on a small part of a bigger whole. They make you think about why the artist chose to paint that picture.

Look at this painting. What can you tell about it? What do you think has happened to make the person hold the animal's paw? What might happen next? Give reasons why you think so.

Look again at the painting. What do you think the artist was trying to show? Why?

Paw
by Darren Harris

"Tian Tian"

READING STRATEGY

Cause and Effect

Develop a strategy for identifying a cause and its effect.

1. **Look for clue words,** such as *since, so,* and *in order to.*

2. **Pay attention to what happens.** Does the text tell about what happened? Then the text is about an *effect.*

3. **Notice why some-thing happened.** If the text tells why something happened, it is about a *cause.*

4. **State a cause and its effect.** Why are pandas endangered? How are people trying to help them?

A Rare Bear

Washington's National Zoo is home to two giant pandas from China. There are only about one thousand of these animals left in the wild.

Why are pandas endangered? One reason is that their home is getting smaller. Pandas eat bamboo, a kind of grass with a thick, woody stem. Pandas can live only where the bamboo grows—in six small forests in the mountains of China.

But China has the largest population of any country in the world—more than a billion people. In order to grow food for so many people, farmers have cleared more and more forest to grow crops. That means less food for the pandas.

Hunting is another reason that pandas are endangered. Even though it is against the law, poachers still hunt pandas for their fur.

A third reason is that female pandas raise only one cub at a time. Since it takes two years for a baby panda to grow up, the mother panda has a cub only every other year. That is not often enough to replace the pandas that are killed by hunters or die for other reasons.

The National Zoo hopes to learn more about pandas by studying them. The more we know, the better the chance we can save them!

"Mei Xiang"

MONGOLIA

Beijing ⊛

CHINA

Wolong Natural Reserve

Xi'an

Yangtze River

Xun River

VIETNAM
LAOS

Panda Range ▪

TIME

FOR KIDS

SPECIAL R

J.J.'s Big Day

A baby whale raised by humans is returned to her ocean home.

J.J.'s Long Journey Home

One winter day, a week-old baby gray whale washed up on a California beach. Anxious scientists examined her. She was sick, hungry, and tired. The scientists didn't know what to feed her. But they knew they had to take care of her. If she got better, they would set the whale free.

Animal-rescue workers brought her to Sea World in San Diego, California. "Suddenly we had this week-old gray whale drop in our laps," says Jim Sumich. He is a scientist who studies whales.

The people at Sea World named the little whale J.J. She needed to gain a lot of weight to become strong. So whale experts at Sea World cooked up some high-fat food. It would take the place of a mother whale's milk. They used heavy cream, clams, and powdered milk. J.J. gulped it down.

ALL PHOTOS: KEN BOHN/SEA WORLD

Cream, clams, and milk were mixed into a "J.J. shake."

The food was poured into a funnel so J.J. could swallow it.

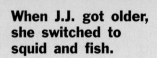

When J.J. got older, she switched to squid and fish.

J.J. began to grow fast! She gained about two pounds every hour. Soon, she was ready to return to her ocean home. There were two big problems, however. J.J. had never had to find her own food before. And it had been a long time since she had been with other whales. "Anything could happen," said Keith Yip. He takes care of animals at Sea World. "Nothing like this had ever been done before."

The Sea World workers made plans to set J.J. free in March. At that time of year, gray whales travel north in the Pacific Ocean. J.J. would have other gray whales to follow. They might teach her where to feed.

1. J.J. is loaded onto a special truck.
2. The truck carries her back to the ocean.
3. J.J. is carefully lowered into the water.

DID YOU KNOW?
WHALE WONDERS

◆ Whales are not fish. They are mammals.

◆ A fish's tail moves side to side. A whale's tail moves up and down.

◆ Most of the larger whales are called baleen whales. Baleen whales have no teeth. They strain out food from the water. Baleen is made from the same stuff as your fingernails.

◆ Other kinds of whales have teeth. They mostly eat fish.

◆ Whales have lungs. They breathe air. Some whales can hold their breath for up to two hours.

J.J. lived in a huge tank at Sea World. You can see how big she is compared to the diver.

How do you move a whale back to the ocean? Very carefully! After all, J.J. weighed 19,200 pounds. She was 31 feet long. So J.J. traveled in a specially made truck. During the 11-mile ride, Keith Yip stroked J.J.'s bumpy nose. He looked into her enormous eyes. "Just saying my good-byes," he said.

A boat then carried J.J. to a safe spot several miles from the beach. J.J. was carefully put into the water. Scientists hope she has joined up with other whales and is doing just fine!

FIND OUT MORE
Visit our website:
www.mhschool.com/reading

*inter*NET
CONNECTION

ILLUSTRATION FOR TIME FOR KIDS BY BOB STAAKE

Based on an article in *TIME FOR KIDS.*

117

Story Questions & Activities

1. Where was J.J. taken to after she was found on a California beach?

2. What helped J.J. gain two pounds every hour? Explain.

3. Why do you think J.J.'s rescuers wanted to return her to the ocean when she was well again?

4. What is the main idea of this selection?

5. What might J.J. tell the blue whale in "Big Blue Whale" about her life at Sea World?

Write a Story

Write a story comparing and contrasting J.J. the Whale's life at Sea World and her life in the ocean. Make at least three comparisons.

118

Design a Lunch Menu

Look up facts about healthy eating. Then design a lunch menu that you would want to eat. Include protein foods, carbohydrates, fruits, and vegetables. Explain why the menu is both good for you and good to eat.

Listen to a Whale Song

Find a recording of whale songs at the library. Listen to it carefully. Then write what you think the whales might be saying to each other. Illustrate your dialogue with a picture of the type of whale on the recording.

Find Out More

Gray whales leave California's coast every March. Learn more about their migration from an encyclopedia or the Internet. Then chart their route on a map and create a bulletin board display.

Pacific Ocean

California

Use a Graph

A graph shows the relationship between changing things.

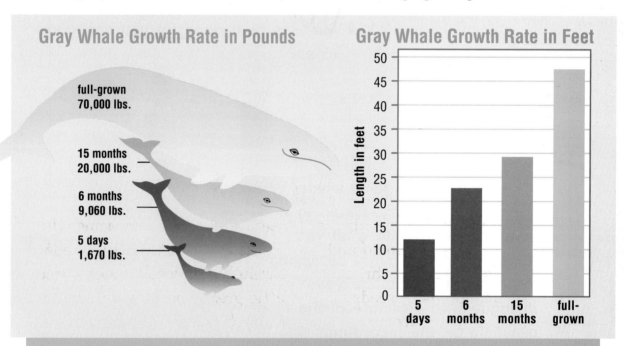

Gray Whale Growth Rate in Pounds

full-grown
70,000 lbs.

15 months
20,000 lbs.

6 months
9,060 lbs.

5 days
1,670 lbs.

Gray Whale Growth Rate in Feet

Length in feet

Use the graphs to answer these questions.

1 What type of graph is used to show the growth rate in feet of a gray whale?

2 How long is a full-grown gray whale and how much does it weigh?

3 About how many pounds does a gray whale gain from 6 months to 15 months?

4 The length of a full-grown gray whale is about double its length at what age?

5 Do you think that all gray whales are 30 feet long and weigh 20,000 pounds when they are 15 months old? Explain.

TEST POWER

DIRECTIONS:

Read the story. Then read each question about the story.

SAMPLE

What Is Falling from the Sky?

"Uncle Nikolo, look at all the seeds with wings!" Antonio and his uncle were walking through the park. Hundreds of seeds were whirling down from the trees. Antonio picked some up and asked, "Can I take these home and put them in my special wooden box?"

Uncle Nikolo said, "If you put these seeds in your box, they will never become trees. All of these maple trees grew from little seeds just like these."

Antonio looked down and said, "I do want the seeds to become trees." Then he smiled. "Can we take a couple of seeds home and plant them?"

Antonio saved three of the seeds and took them home. He planted and watered the seeds carefully. Six weeks later, three little green shoots were poking through the dirt in the yard.

1 Shoots poked through the dirt because—

○ the seeds were growing

○ an animal moved them

○ the dirt was old

○ the shoots were toys

2 How did Antonio feel as he watched seeds fall?

○ Scared

○ Happy

○ Lazy

○ Tired

121

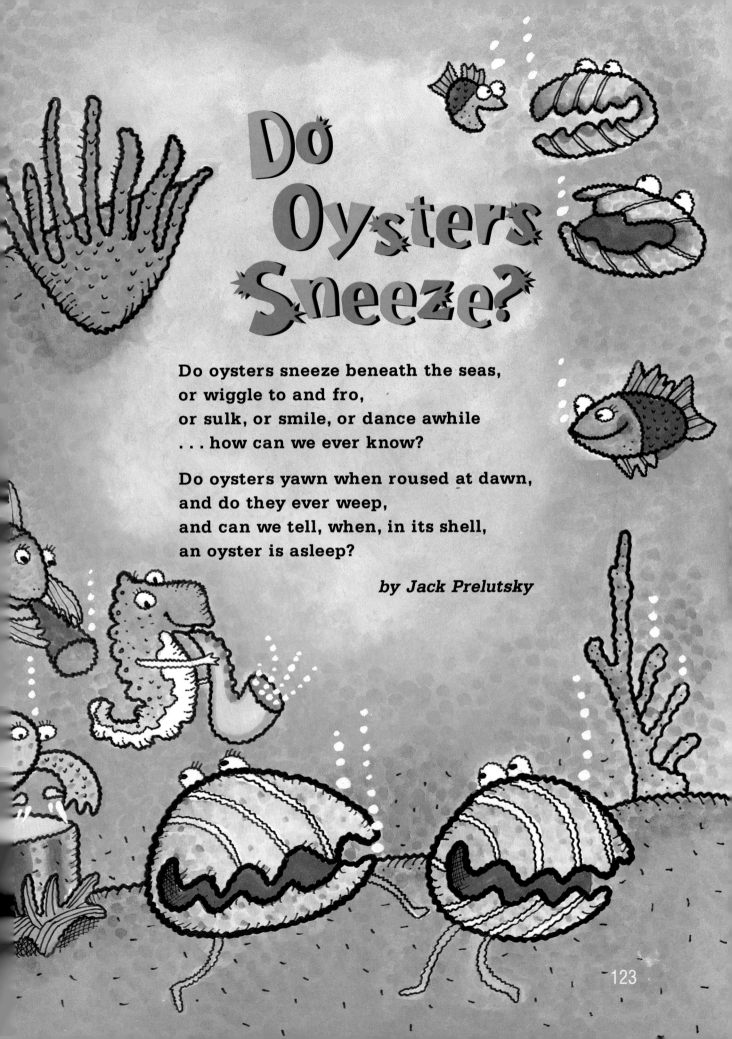

Do Oysters Sneeze?

Do oysters sneeze beneath the seas,
or wiggle to and fro,
or sulk, or smile, or dance awhile
. . . how can we ever know?

Do oysters yawn when roused at dawn,
and do they ever weep,
and can we tell, when, in its shell,
an oyster is asleep?

by Jack Prelutsky

Think It Through

I Can

I can
be anything
I can
do anything
I can
think
anything
big
or tall
OR
high or low
W I D E
or narrow
fast or slow
because I
CAN
and
I
WANT
TO!

by Mari Evans

This is a Native American wolf mask. It was made by an artist on the western coast of Canada over a hundred years ago.

Look at this mask. What can you tell about the person who made it? What do you think the mask was used for? Why do you think people made masks of certain animals?

Pretend that you are going to wear this mask. How would it make you feel? Why?

Makah Wolf Mask, late 19th century
The Burke Museum of Natural History and Culture
Seattle, Washington

Judgments and Decisions

Develop a strategy for making judgments and decisions.

1 **Study the character's actions.** What does the character do?

2 **Figure out why the character** acts that way.

3 **Think about what you would do.** Was there a different way to act?

4 **Look at the results** of the character's actions. Did the actions hurt or help?

5 **Make judgments.** Should Kevin have gone into the forest? Was his decision to hold up the mirror a good one? Explain your answers.

Kevin and the BEAR

One summer, Kevin visited his grandfather, who lived in a cottage at the edge of a forest.

The first morning, Kevin jumped out of bed and looked out the cottage window. "The forest is so beautiful!" he cried out. "I can't wait to explore it."

"Don't go too far from the cottage," Grandpa warned him. "A bear lives in the forest. Be careful."

After breakfast, Kevin joined the squirrels and chipmunks and rabbits. He happily followed them as they ran through the thick forest of maple trees and evergreens.

Kevin did not realize how far he had gone. Suddenly, a bear growled in the distance. Without thinking, Kevin turned and ran toward the cottage.

The cottage was not too far. Just in time, Kevin reached the cottage and slammed the door.

Suddenly, Kevin saw the bear at the window. He noticed Grandpa's big mirror. He grabbed it and held it up in front of the window. The angry bear *thought* he saw another angry bear! He turned back and never returned.

Grandpa had been out chopping wood. When he came in, Kevin told him all about the bear.

"Good thinking!" said Grandpa. "You scared that bear away for a *long* time."

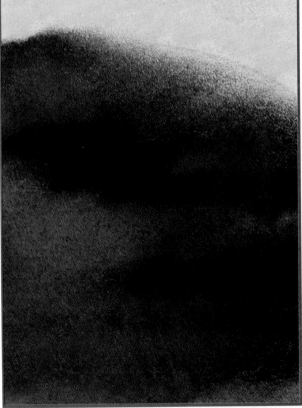

Once, long ago, there was a woman who lived alone in the country with her three children, Shang, Tao, and Paotze. On the day of their grandmother's birthday, the good mother set off to see her, leaving the three children at home.

Before she left, she said, "Be good while I am away, my heart-loving children; I will not return tonight. Remember to close the door tight at sunset and latch it well."

But an old wolf lived nearby and saw the good mother leave. At dusk, disguised as an old woman, he came up to the house of the children and knocked on the door twice: bang, bang.

Shang, who was the eldest, said through the latched door, "Who is it?"

"My little jewels," said the wolf, "this is your grandmother, your Po Po."

"Po Po!" Shang said. "Our mother has gone to visit you!"

The wolf acted surprised. "To visit me? I have not met her along the way. She must have taken a different route."

"Po Po!" Shang said. "How is it that you come so late?"

The wolf answered, "The journey is long, my children, and the day is short."

Shang listened through the door. "Po Po," she said, "why is your voice so low?"

"Your grandmother has caught a cold, good children, and it is dark and windy out here. Quickly open up, and let your Po Po come in," the cunning wolf said.

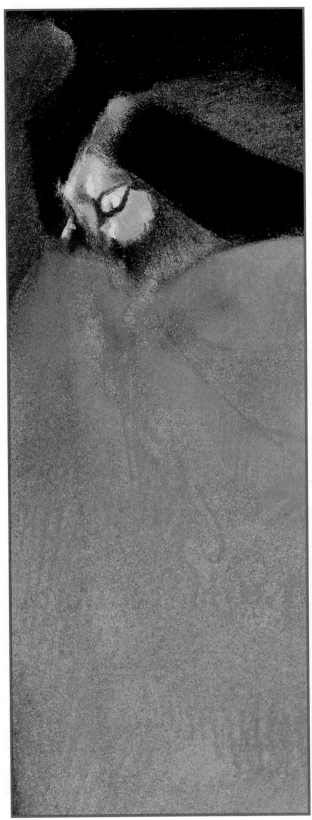

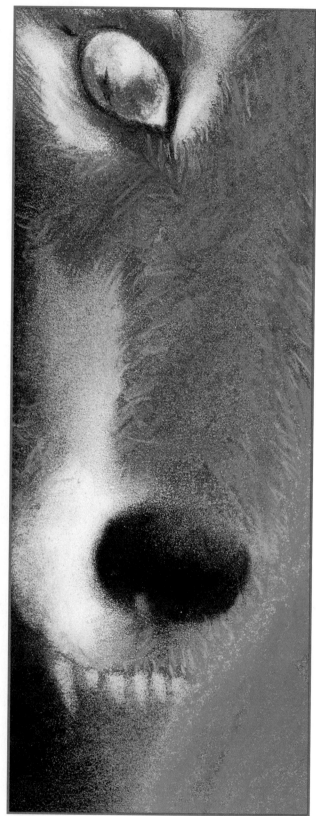

132

Tao and Paotze could
not wait. One unlatched the
door and the other opened it.
They shouted, "Po Po, Po Po,
come in!"

At the moment he entered
the door, the wolf blew out the
candle.

"Po Po," Shang asked, "why
did you blow out the candle?
The room is now dark."

The wolf did not answer.

Tao and Paotze rushed to
their Po Po and wished to be
hugged. The old wolf held Tao.
"Good child, you are so plump."
He embraced Paotze. "Good
child, you have grown to be
so sweet."

Soon the old wolf pretended
to be sleepy. He yawned. "All
the chicks are in the coop," he
said. "Po Po is sleepy too."

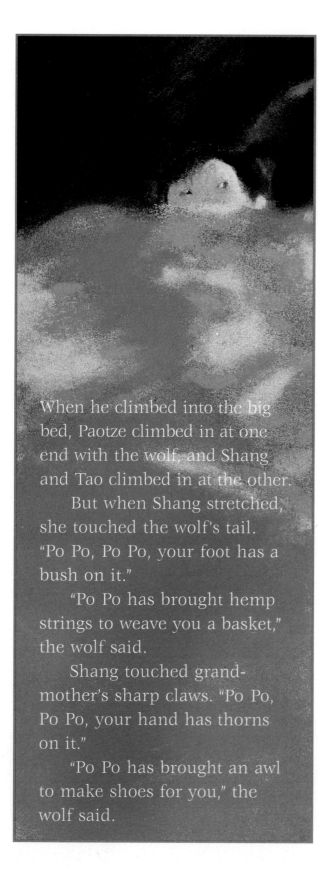

When he climbed into the big bed, Paotze climbed in at one end with the wolf, and Shang and Tao climbed in at the other.

But when Shang stretched, she touched the wolf's tail. "Po Po, Po Po, your foot has a bush on it."

"Po Po has brought hemp strings to weave you a basket," the wolf said.

Shang touched grandmother's sharp claws. "Po Po, Po Po, your hand has thorns on it."

"Po Po has brought an awl to make shoes for you," the wolf said.

At once, Shang lit the light and the wolf blew it out again, but Shang had seen the wolf's hairy face.

"Po Po, Po Po," she said, for she was not only the eldest, she was the most clever, "you must be hungry. Have you eaten gingko nuts?"

"What is gingko?" the wolf asked.

"Gingko is soft and tender, like the skin of a baby. One taste and you will live forever," Shang said, "and the nuts grow on the top of the tree just outside the door."

The wolf gave a sigh. "Oh, dear. Po Po is old, her bones have become brittle. No longer can she climb trees."

"Good Po Po, we can pick some for you," Shang said.

The wolf was delighted.

Shang jumped out of bed and Tao and Paotze came with her to the gingko tree. There, Shang told her sisters about the wolf and all three climbed up the tall tree.

The wolf waited and waited. Plump Tao did not come back. Sweet Paotze did not come back. Shang did not come back, and no one brought any nuts from the gingko tree. At last the wolf shouted, "Where are you, children?"

"Po Po," Shang called out, "we are on the top of the tree eating gingko nuts."

"Good children," the wolf begged, "pluck some for me."

"But Po Po, gingko is magic only when it is plucked directly from the tree. You must come and pluck it from the tree yourself."

The wolf came outside and paced back and forth under the tree where he heard the three children eating the gingko nuts at the top. "Oh, Po Po, these nuts are so tasty! The skin so tender," Shang said. The wolf's mouth began to water for a taste.

Finally, Shang, the eldest and most clever child, said, "Po Po, Po Po, I have a plan. At the door there is a big basket. Behind it is a rope. Tie the rope to the basket, sit in the basket and throw the other end to me. I can pull you up."

The wolf was overjoyed and fetched the basket and the rope, then threw one end of the rope to the top of the tree. Shang caught the rope and began to pull the basket up and up.

Halfway she let go of the rope, and the basket and the wolf fell to the ground.

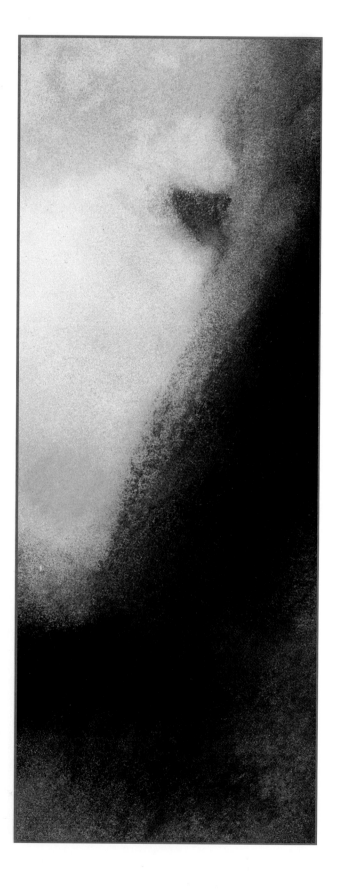

143

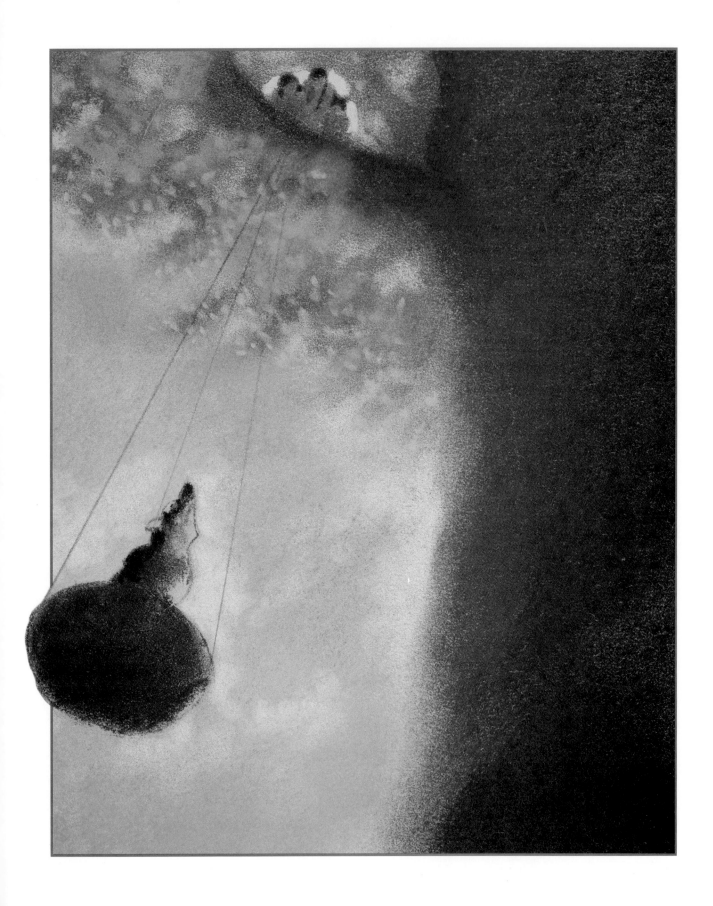

"I am so small and weak, Po Po," Shang pretended. "I could not hold the rope alone."

"This time I will help," Tao said. "Let us do it again."

The wolf had only one thought in his mind: to taste a gingko nut. He climbed into the basket again. Now Shang and Tao pulled the rope on the basket together, higher and higher.

Again, they let go, and again the wolf tumbled down, down, and bumped his head.

The wolf was furious. He growled and cursed. "We could not hold the rope, Po Po," Shang said, "but only one gingko nut and you will be well again."

"I shall give a hand to my sisters this time," Paotze, the youngest, said. "This time we shall not fail."

Now the children pulled the rope with all of their strength. As they pulled they sang, "Hei yo, hei yo," and the basket rose straight up, higher than the first time, higher than the second time, higher and higher and higher until it nearly reached the top of the tree. When the wolf reached out, he could almost touch the highest branch.

But at that moment, Shang coughed and they all let go of the rope, and the basket fell down and down and down. Not only did the wolf bump his head, but he broke his heart to pieces.

"Po Po," Shang shouted, but there was no answer.

"Po Po," Tao shouted, but there was no answer.

"Po Po," Paotze shouted. There was still no answer. The children climbed to the branches just above the wolf and saw that he was truly dead. Then they climbed down, went into the house, closed the door, locked the door with the latch and fell peacefully asleep.

On the next day, their mother returned with baskets of food from their real Po Po, and the three sisters told her the story of the Po Po who had come.

MEET

Ed Young

While growing up in China, Ed Young loved to hear old Chinese folk tales. One favorite was the tale of Lon Po Po. As he listened, he never imagined that someday he would write the tale in English, add his own drawings, and win the Caldecott Medal.

Young remembers that he nearly always had a pencil in his hand when he was a boy. "I drew everything that happened to cross my mind: airplanes, people, a tall ship that my father was very proud of, a hunter and a bird dog that came out of my head." He kept on drawing when he moved to New York City and got a job. During his lunch hours, he sat in Central Park Zoo and drew animals.

One day Young was told to see an editor at a large publishing company. He carried a shopping bag containing animal drawings. The editor liked his work and asked him to do the drawings for *The Mean Mouse and Other Mean Stories*.

Since then, Young has drawn pictures for over fifty books, five of which he wrote himself.

Story Questions & Activities

1. Whom did the wolf pretend to be?

2. When did Shang realize the wolf was not really her grandmother?

3. Do you think Shang is clever? Explain.

4. What is the story mostly about?

5. Compare Shang and Fernando Espino. How did each character find a clever solution to a problem?

Write an Advice Column

Pretend that Shang and her sisters have asked for your advice on how to get rid of the wolf. Write a response to their letter. Include a step-by-step plan.

Design a Kite

Kites were invented in China. Draw the outline of a kite on a large piece of paper. Cut out your kite and attach yarn to the bottom. Then decorate it with colored markers. With the rest of the class, create a kite display.

Lift With a Lever

In "Lon Po Po," three little girls are able to lift a heavy wolf. You can lift heavy objects, too. Set the middle of a ruler on top of a cardboard tube. Place a heavy book on one end of the ruler. Then press down on the other end of the ruler.

Find Out More

What other versions of "Red Riding Hood" can you find in the fairy tale section of the library? How are they like or different from "Lon Po Po"?

155

STUDY SKILLS

Read a Newspaper

A newspaper prints news stories that give **facts** and often contain **opinions**, too. A fact is a statement that can be checked and proven true. An opinion tells how a person feels. A good reader must learn to tell the difference.

May 2, 1999

Gray Wolf Escapes From Washington Zoo

by Carrie Chiu

Last night at 11:30 P.M., a guard at the Washington Zoo saw a wolf escape. Evidently, the door to the wolf's cage had not been shut all the way.

"I've never seen anything run so fast," said the guard.

The guard called a zookeeper who called the police. After several hours, a police officer spotted the wolf in a local park. The zookeeper was able to catch the wolf by placing some meat inside a crate. When the wolf entered the crate, the zookeeper shut the door. The wolf was back at the zoo by 2:30 A.M.

"I'm glad we found him," said the zookeeper. "He wouldn't have hurt anybody, but I'm glad he's back."

Use the news story to answer these questions.

1 What is the headline?

2 Who wrote the article?

3 A good news story answers the following questions: **who**, **what**, **when**, **where**, **how**. In this news story, what facts are given for each question?

4 What are two opinions in the article?

5 How could you check the facts in this news story?

156

TEST POWER

Test Tip

If you do not understand the story, go back and read it again carefully.

DIRECTIONS:

Read the story. Then read each question about the story.

SAMPLE

Life in a Fishing Village

Tika grew up in a fishing village in Greece. She smelled the sea every day as she walked to school.

Tika's father was a fisherman. Every day when Tika went to school, her father put the big nets and the barrels of bait in his boat. Then he fished all day. After school, Tika met her father on the docks. She spent many hours helping him.

Tika had to do many <u>tasks</u>. She had to hang the fishing nets out to dry. Sometimes Tika's father asked her to help him clean the boat. She liked to do this most of all because she loved being on the boat with her father. She knew that one day he would let her drive the boat.

1 What is this story mostly about?

○ When Tika drives the boat

○ How to fish in Greece

○ How Tika helped her father

○ Why people live in a fishing village

2 In this story, <u>tasks</u> are —

○ jobs

○ homework

○ fishing poles

○ lunches

This photograph shows a scene from a movie. Sometimes movies show things that could not happen in real life.

Look at the setting of this picture. What can you tell about it? What is happening in the picture? What parts could not happen in real life? Give reasons why you think so.

Look at the picture again. How can you tell this movie was made a long time ago?

King Kong atop the Empire State Building from the movie *King Kong*, 1933

Fact and Nonfact

Develop a strategy for identifying facts and nonfacts.

1 **As you read,** ask yourself what statements can be proved. These are facts.

2 **Find details** in the article that support each statement. Can the details be proved?

3 **Identify statements** that cannot be proved. These are not facts.

4 **Look at the information in the chart.** Are any of the statements not facts?

DO ELEPHANTS EVER FORGET?

There is a popular saying, "An elephant never forgets." Studies have shown that this is untrue. If we change the sentence to "An elephant almost never forgets," then it becomes true.

The elephant has a large brain and is one of the smartest animals on land. It has an excellent memory and hardly ever forgets its experiences. Scientists have proven this by studying elephant behavior over many years.

A Good Memory

Because it has a good memory, an elephant can be taught to do many things. A trainer can sit on an elephant and slowly teach it to follow signals.

The trainer gives signals by touching the elephant behind its ears. An elephant can remember the signals that tell it to stand, turn around, walk forward, walk backward, and kneel.

An elephant can also remember spoken signals. It can learn as many as forty voice commands. That's a pretty good memory!

Did You Know?

- An elephant is the heaviest animal on land. It has the largest ears and tusks of any animal.

- An elephant is the only animal with a trunk for a nose. It breathes and smells with it.

- An elephant also uses its trunk to pick up things. It can hold a huge 600-pound log or a tiny peanut.

- An elephant's favorite thing is to play in water. It loves to spray water from its trunk.

ANIMAL FACT/
Animal Fable

by Seymour Simon

Illustrated by Diane de Groat

We all know *facts* about animals—things that are true. But from watching animals and reading stories and tales about them, we may have some beliefs that are not true. We may believe in *fables* rather than facts.

In this science selection, decide whether each statement about an animal is a fact or a fable. Then turn the page to find out what scientists have discovered.

A turtle can walk out of its shell.

Fable When people find an empty turtle shell on the ground, they may think a turtle left it behind and moved into a new one. But that is not true. A turtle can no more walk out of its shell than you can walk away from your ribs.

A turtle's shell is not just a house it lives in. The shell is really part of the turtle's body. You should not try to take a turtle out of its shell. If you do, the turtle will die. The empty shells you may find on the ground are the remains of turtles that have died.

Crickets tell the temperature with their chirps.

FACT Crickets are animals whose body temperatures change with the temperature around them. On a hot day, crickets chirp so rapidly that it is hard to count the number of chirps. But on a cool day, crickets chirp much more slowly. We can then easily count the times they chirp.

Some people say they can use the number of chirps to find the exact temperature. That's not always possible. A cricket's chirping depends upon its age and health as well as on the temperature.

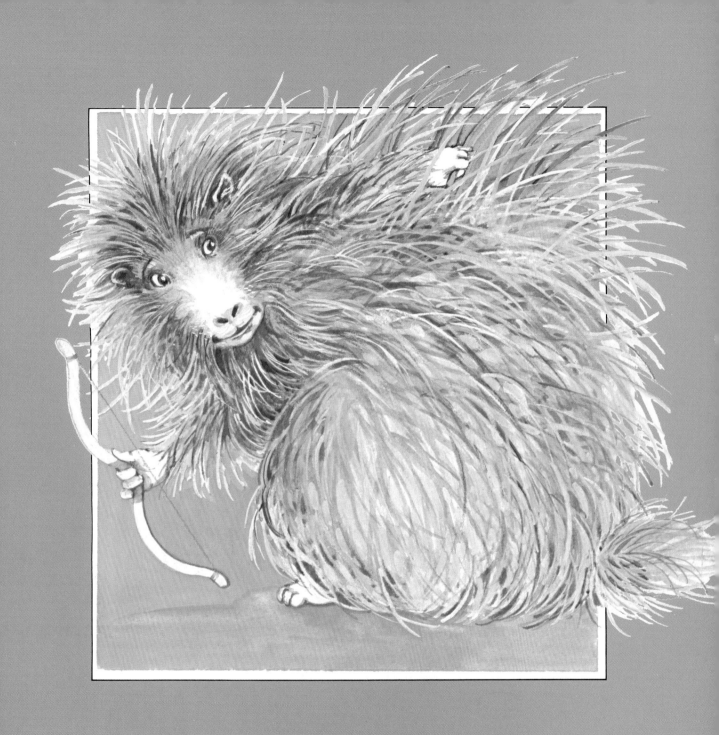

Porcupines shoot their quills.

Fable   Porcupines cannot really shoot their quills. A porcupine's quills are sharp and have barbs like tiny hooks. The tip of a quill shown here has been magnified many times. When the quill sinks into an animal it becomes stuck and is left behind.

Porcupines use their quills to protect themselves. If an animal or person bothers a porcupine, the quills stand on end. The porcupine turns around and backs up to his enemy. Few animals bother a porcupine a second time.

Dogs talk with their tails.

FACT

We know dogs don't use words to talk, but their tails can tell us how they feel. When a dog wags its tail from side to side, the dog is happy and playful. But when a dog wags its tail up and down, it may be because it has done something wrong and expects to be punished.

If a dog keeps its tail straight up, be careful. That is the signal that it may attack. Don't run, just back away slowly.

Ostriches hide their heads in the sand.

Fable There is a well-known fable that ostriches stick their heads in the sand when they are frightened. Here's how the fable may have started. When ostriches see an enemy, they sometimes drop down and stretch out their necks along the ground. This makes it more difficult for the enemy to see them. To a person watching an ostrich, it may look as if the ostrich has buried its head in the ground.

An ostrich may not be very smart, but it is not dumb. When an enemy comes close, the ostrich gets up from the ground and runs away.

Goats will eat almost anything.

FACT Goats will eat almost anything they can find. They even seem to eat tin cans. But they are not really eating the metal can; they are chewing the label to get at the glue underneath.

Though goats eat string and paper, they would rather eat fruit, vegetables, grass, and leaves of plants. They are not quite the "garbage cans" some people think they are.

MEET SEYMOUR SIMON

Are you full of questions about the world? Do you wonder why fall weather turns some leaves red and others yellow? Is it a puzzle to you how a heavy ship can float? Science writer Seymour Simon likes questions like these. He says, "It's questions . . . that occur to me and that have been asked of me by children . . . that make me want to write science books."

Simon was a science teacher for twenty-three years. (He must have answered a million questions during those years!) Now he writes books full-time. Nearly 150 books with his name on the front are stacked on his shelves. More than fifty of them have received awards from the National Science Teachers Association. Among his award-winning books are *Mirror Magic, Stars,* and *The Moon.*

To answer questions for his books, Simon says he has "collected rocks, dug under rotting logs, tramped through swamps." He has also shared his home with earthworms, gerbils, ants, and crickets. He says about his books, "Sometimes I'll provide an answer, but more often I'll suggest an activity or an experiment that will let a child answer a question by trying it out."

Story Questions & Activities

1. What do turtles use their shells for?

2. Do ostriches really hide their heads in the sand? Explain.

3. When a dog wags its tail from side to side, is it happy or angry?

4. What is the main idea of this selection?

5. Pretend Seymour Simon wants to write about wolves in "Animal Fact/Animal Fable." If he were to interview Shang, what might she tell him about wolves?

Write an Animal Report

Choose one of the animals from the selection. Write a report about it. Use facts and supporting details.

Make a Mobile

Choose your favorite wild animal and create a mobile. Draw the shape of the animal and cut it out. Color in the animal and add eyes and a mouth. Write three facts on file cards. Punch a hole at the top of each card and the picture. Tie the picture and the cards to a hanger using different lengths of string.

Design a Mask

Find a picture of your favorite animal. Draw the outline of its head on a piece of poster board. Cut the head out and then carefully cut holes for eyes. Staple a piece of yarn to either side of the mask. Then use colored markers or paints to decorate it.

Find Out More

Do cats really have nine lives? Does an elephant never forget? Think of more stories you have heard about animals and find out if they are facts or fables. Look in science books and encyclopedias to find the facts.

Study Skills

Read a Newspaper

In this selection, Seymour Simon helped you to tell fact from fable. Newspaper articles are usually a mixture of fact and opinion. Good readers need to be able to identify the facts.

June 9, 1999

Maplewood Library May Close

by Amanda Page

Mayor Williams announced that the Maplewood Library may soon close. She spoke to reporters on the steps of Town Hall.

"We do not have enough money to keep the library open. If we don't raise the money, the library will close in six months. It is a sad day for Maplewood," said the mayor.

Bob Lee, a businessman, has started a Save the Library drive. He and other concerned citizens are planning ways to raise money.

"Maplewood needs a library. We must save it," said Mr. Lee.

Use the newspaper article to answer these questions.

1. Where did the Mayor speak to reporters?

2. What is one fact that the Mayor told the reporters?

3. What is one opinion she gave?

4. Is what Bob Lee said a fact or opinion?

5. In your opinion should the Maplewood Library be closed?

176

TEST POWER

Test Tip

Sometimes it helps to tell the story again in your own words.

DIRECTIONS:
Read the story. Then read each question about the story.

SAMPLE

Golf

Golf is a game that is played on a large piece of land called a golf course. A golfer uses a golf club to hit a small ball into a hole in the ground.

Golf started as a sport in the country of Scotland. It is usually played in groups of four people.

In many sports, the winner is the person with the highest score. In golf, the winner is the person with the lowest score. Players get a point every time they hit their golf ball. Good golfers get the ball into the hole with just a few hits. Some golfers even make a hole-in-one. They hit the ball once and it goes in the hole!

1 Which is a FACT in the story?

○ Golf started in England.

○ Golf is played in groups of five people.

○ Golf is played on a golf course.

○ The winner has the highest score.

2 What happens when a golfer gets the ball in the hole with one swing?

○ The game is over.

○ The golfer gets a hole-in-one.

○ The golfer gets a higher score.

○ The game is played again.

Stories in Art

Some artists set out to tell about a moment in history. By making a picture of it, they help bring history to life.

Look at the picture. Read the title. What information does the title give you? What do you think is the main idea of the picture? What is the boy doing?

Close your eyes. What do you remember about the picture? Why?

178

Franklin's Experiment in Electricity
by Currier and Ives

Main Idea

Develop a strategy for finding the main idea.

1 **Read the title.** What clues does the title give you about the article?

2 **Identify who or what** the article is mostly about. What is the main thing that is being said?

3 **Look for details.** How do they relate to the main idea?

4 **Are there charts or maps** with supporting details?

5 **State the main idea in your own words.** What is interesting about Sybil Ludington?

Sybil Ludington's Daring Ride

Sybil Ludington was born in 1761. The Ludington family lived in Fredericksburg, a city in Dutchess County, New York.

Sybil's father was an important man. He owned a mill and served as sheriff. He was also a colonel in the army and in charge of a regiment of soldiers. He and his soldiers were fighting in the war against the British.

One rainy night in April, 1777, a messenger arrived. He had ridden hard from Danbury, Connecticut, about 17 miles away. The British Army was burning the town of Danbury! The people of that city needed help from Colonel Ludington and his soldiers.

But it was spring, and the soldiers had returned to their homes to plant their fields. Who could get word to them? Colonel Ludington asked Sybil to go.

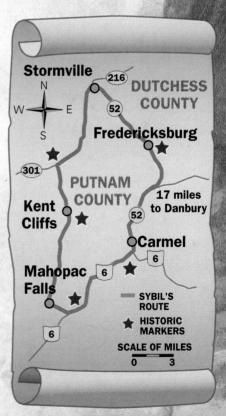

Sixteen-year-old Sybil galloped off into the night. She rode on dark and dangerous roads, where robbers sometimes lay in wait. Thanks to Sybil's bravery, by dawn almost all of her father's regiment was at his house, ready to march to Danbury. Today, many people compare Sybil's journey with that of Paul Revere's famous ride.

Meet Aliki

Aliki started drawing at an early age. By the time she was in kindergarten, her talent was so strong that her teacher noticed her pictures. "Such a fuss was made over them that the course of my life was decided," Aliki says.

Aliki has written and illustrated more than 60 books. Her books are about everything from dinosaurs, fossils, and mummies to how a book is made. When Aliki writes stories, she uses her family and her own experiences for ideas.

Aliki thinks carefully about how she will illustrate a book. She says, "The pictures add to the words and make them more important."

Aliki lives in England with her family. Among the biographies she has written are *The Story of Johnny Appleseed* and *George and the Cherry Tree*. Some of her award-winning books are *At Mary Bloom's, Corn Is Maize: The Gift of the Indians,* and *Mummies Made in Egypt.*

The Many Lives of Benjamin Franklin

Written down and illustrated by
Aliki

The Free Library of Philadelphia - founded by Benjamin Franklin in 1731.

*B*enjamin Franklin was born with just one life. But as he grew, his curiosity, his sense of humor, and his brilliant mind, turned him into a man with many lives.

Benjamin Franklin was born in Boston in 1706. His mother and his father, who was a candlemaker, had many children. But they saw Ben was special. He was curious. He loved books. And even as a child, he was full of bright ideas.

Boston 1706

Ben's paddles were wooden, with a hole for his thumb. He made paddles for his feet, too.

*B*en was always thinking—even at play. He liked to swim, and tried different ways. Once he made paddles so he could go faster.

Another time, when he was flying his kite near a pond, he had another idea. He went for a swim holding on to the kite string. Just as he thought, the kite pulled him across the water.

Ben loved school, but his parents did not have the money for him to continue.

After only two years, he had to leave and choose a trade. It was decided that Ben would learn to be a printer like his brother, James. So when he was twelve, Ben was sent to live with him. Ben learned quickly. He worked long, hard hours. Still, he found time to read every book he could borrow, and saved the money he earned to buy more.

Ben's job as an apprentice was to clean and sort type, sweep the floor, and sell newspapers.

Ben spent nights and Sundays reading and practicing his writing.

At the shop, Ben wanted to do more than just help print his brother's newspaper. He wanted to write in it, too. So he thought of a way.

James began finding mysterious letters under the office door. They were signed "Silence Dogood." Silence wrote such funny stories, clever essays, and poetry, James printed them. In fact, they helped him sell more newspapers. Little did he know that Silence Dogood was his little brother Ben.

But when James found out, he was angry. Ben was not allowed to write anymore. He decided to go somewhere else, where he could write. So when he was 17, he left James and Boston.

Ben worked very hard and even delivered his packages himself.

Ben went to Philadelphia to start a life of his own. He found a job with a printer. He read and collected more books. He worked and saved until at last he bought his own shop. Now he could print his own newspaper and all the letters he wished.

$\mathcal{A}$ few years later, Ben met and married a young girl named Deborah Read. Deborah worked hard, too. She managed their new house, and her own general store next to Ben's print shop. Before long they had two children to help them.

WILLIAM was the oldest.

FRANCIS was born in 1732. When he was four, he got very sick and died.

Baby SARAH was called "Sally" by her father.

*B*en's newspaper was a great success. Then he began printing a yearly calendar called Poor Richard's Almanack. The booklet was full of advice, news, and information. What made it even more special were the wise, witty sayings of Poor Richard. Year after year, people bought the almanac. It made Ben famous.

Meanwhile, Benjamin Franklin was busy living other lives. He loved Philadelphia. It was a new city full of promise, and Benjamin was there at the right time. He started a club called the Junto, where friends met to discuss books and ideas.

Benjamin Franklin pretended Richard Saunders wrote the almanac.

"Poor Richard" was Richard Saunders, a poor astrologer who liked to spend his time gazing at the stars. His wife nagged him to get to work and make some money, so he decided to please her. That is why he wrote his almanac.

SUNRISE   SUNSET

Poor   Richard's   Sayings :

Early to bed and early to rise, makes a man healthy, wealthy, and wise.

Beware of little expenses. A small leak will sink a great ship.

'Tis hard for an empty bag to stand upright.

Up, sluggard, and waste not life.

A word to the wise is enough.

At the working man's house, hunger looks in but dares not enter.

Every little makes a mickle.

One today is worth two tomorrows.

191

*H*e lent out his books, and soon others did the same. This began the first free lending library in America. He found new ways to light the streets, and to have them cleaned and paved, too. He started a police force, a fire department, a hospital, and an Academy. He helped make laws. Philadelphia became as famous as Benjamin Franklin.

Benjamin Franklin in his fireman's helmet.

A lamplighter walked through the streets at dusk lighting lamps.

By the time he was forty-two, Benjamin Franklin had enough money from his printing to live in comfort with his family. He gave up the shop to spend all his time with his ideas. A new life began. Ben started scientific experiments, and soon became a master. He was the first to prove lightning was electricity. One day, during a thunderstorm, he tried a dangerous experiment with a kite and a key, and found he was right. He realized how to protect houses from lightning, and invented the lightning rod.

Benjamin Franklin's Dangerous Kite Experiment

He attached a pointed metal rod to the kite.

He tied a silk cord to the kite string and a key to the cord.

He and his son, William, took shelter. Lightning struck the rod.

He touched the wet key and felt a shock. Electricity had traveled down the kite string to the key. The silk cord stopped it from going further.

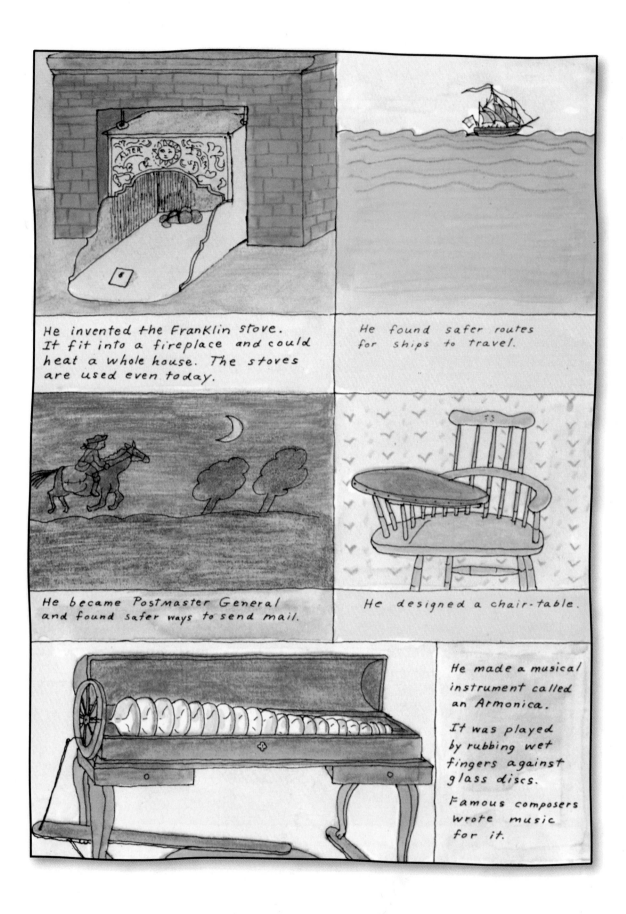

He invented the Franklin stove. It fit into a fireplace and could heat a whole house. The stoves are used even today.

He found safer routes for ships to travel.

He became Postmaster General and found safer ways to send mail.

He designed a chair-table.

He made a musical instrument called an Armonica.

It was played by rubbing wet fingers against glass discs.

Famous composers wrote music for it.

He experimented in his garden and found better ways to grow crops.

He found out that black cloth keeps one warmer than white by laying pieces of cloth in the snow. After some time, the black cloth was warmed by the sun and sank into the snow. The white didn't.

Benjamin Franklin made many discoveries in his lifetime, but he refused money for them. He said his ideas belonged to everyone. He wrote them down and they were translated into many languages. He became the best known man in America.

More than anything, Benjamin hoped people would listen to his most important idea—freedom for his country. For at that time, America was an English colony. He—and others—did not want to be ruled by England any longer.

Pennsylvania State House, now called Independence Hall, in 1776.

Benjamin Franklin, Thomas Jefferson, John Adams, John Hancock, and 52 others, signed the Declaration of Independence in Philadelphia on July 4, 1776.

$\mathcal{H}$e was sent to England to seek independence for his country. For eighteen long years, Benjamin stayed there and worked for that goal. In 1775, he returned to Philadelphia, sad and disappointed. His wife had died. War with England had begun, and America was still not free.

Yet he persisted. Benjamin Franklin and other great Americans helped Thomas Jefferson write the Declaration of Independence. They were determined to be free. But they knew they would first have to fight a long, terrible war. And they did.

General George Washington led many battles during the Revolutionary War.

$\mathcal{B}$ut they needed help. Benjamin Franklin was old and weary when again he sailed away. This time he went to ask for aid from the King of France.

Benjamin was greeted as a hero. People in France knew about him and his inventions, and they loved him. Finally, the King agreed. With his help, the war with England was won. America was free at last.

In 1781 the war ended. The Liberty Bell in Independence Hall rang out.

In France, he visited King Louis XVI and Queen Marie Antoinette. Though everyone wore fancy clothes and powdered wigs, Benjamin Franklin did not. Everyone was impressed with the inventor's plain clothes and simple ways.

On September 13, 1785, his ship entered Philadelphia Harbor. Bells rang, cannons boomed, and hundreds of people waited to welcome Benjamin home.

*B*enjamin Franklin had served abroad long enough. He wanted to spend his last years at home. When he finally returned from France, it was 1785. He thought he had been forgotten.

But he was not forgotten. He was greeted with wild celebrations. He saw his country still needed him. He became the first governor of Pennsylvania and helped write the Constitution of the United States.

On September 17, 1787, Benjamin Franklin and the other great writers of the Constitution signed the document on which all laws of the United States are based.

Benjamin Franklin lived eighty-four years. He left the world his inventions, his ideas, his wisdom and his wit. He lived many lives for us all.

Story Questions & Activities

1. What city did Ben Franklin move to after he left Boston?

2. What are three important things that Ben Franklin did?

3. Why did Aliki call this selection "The Many Lives of Benjamin Franklin"?

4. What is the main idea of this selection?

5. What does Marcy in "City Green" have in common with Ben Franklin?

Write a Brochure

Create a brochure describing some of Ben Franklin's inventions. Give as many details as possible about the inventions.

Do an Experiment

Ben Franklin found that dark colors attract heat better than light colors. Try this experiment. Take two paper cups. Place four ice cubes in each one. Tape a square of black paper over one cup, and a square of white paper over the other. Put both cups in direct sunlight. Which cup of ice melts the fastest?

Make a Book of Sayings

Ben Franklin had many sayings such as, "A penny saved is a penny earned," and "Never put off until tomorrow what you can do today." Make a book of your favorite sayings and illustrate it.

Find Out More

Benjamin Franklin is known for his many inventions and discoveries. Find out about another inventor and what he or she invented. Then draw a picture of the invention and tell how it is useful to people.

203

Follow Directions

Static electricity is the crackle when you comb your hair and the tingle when you take off a wool sweater. The lightning that flashes in a thunderstorm is static electricity, too. You can conduct a simple science experiment to show the effect of static electricity.

Follow directions 1–3. Then answer questions 4–5.

1 Cut a piece of aluminum foil into five small pieces. Lay the pieces on a table.

2 Quickly move a comb through your hair.

3 Hold the teeth of the comb above the foil pieces. Do not touch them with the comb. What do you predict will happen?

4 Was your prediction correct?

5 What did you learn from this experiment?

TEST POWER

DIRECTIONS:

Read the story. Then read each question about the story.

SAMPLE

What Did Carl Learn?

At the zoo, Carl said to the zookeeper, "These wolves look and act just like my pet dog, Champ."

The zookeeper nodded. "That's because your dog was once a wolf just like these animals."

Carl gasped. "I've had Champ since he was a pup! He was never a wolf!"

The zookeeper laughed. "I mean that the dogs we keep as pets today are related to the wolf."

"So, would Champ make friends and hunt with a pack of wolves?" Carl asked.

"He wouldn't really know what to do with wolves. It has been thousands of years since one of Champ's relatives lived in the wild," the zookeeper explained.

1 This story is mostly about—

   ○ the food Champ eats

   ○ how dogs are related to wolves

   ○ a wolf who is trapped

   ○ dogs that do tricks

2 What was Carl doing at the beginning of the story?

   ○ Walking his dog, Champ

   ○ Asking for directions

   ○ Looking at the bears

   ○ Talking to the zookeeper

Stories in Art

When you first look at this painting, you might see lots of shapes. If you look again, you might see that some of the shapes are storm clouds.

What can you tell about this painting? What kind of setting is this? What details do you notice? How would you describe this painting to a friend?

Look at the painting again. What colors did the artist use? What does this painting make you think of?

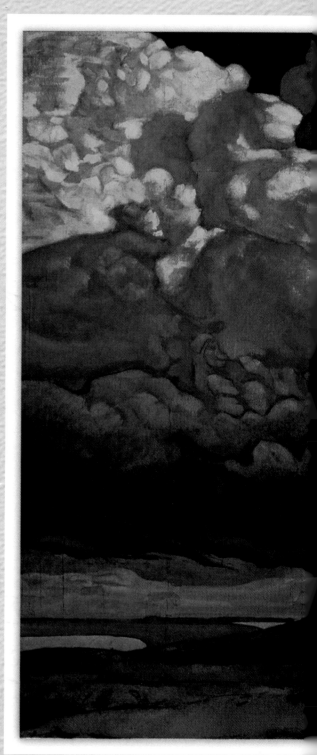

Celestial Combat by Nikolai Roerich
Russian State Museum, St. Petersburg, Russia

Summarize

Develop a strategy for summarizing information.

1 **Read the title.** What does it tell you about the subject of the article?

2 **Decide what is being said.** What is the main idea?

3 **Look for important details.** Which details are the most important pieces of information?

4 **Summarize.** In your own words, tell why it sometimes rains cats and dogs.

Raining Cats and Dogs

Have you ever heard anyone say that it was raining cats and dogs? If you had, you probably thought that they were joking.

Most of the time they are. But not always. Sometimes it really does rain cats and dogs. Fish, too.

Thousands of fish rained down on Marksville, Louisiana, on October 23, 1947. There have been similar "rains" throughout history. They have included eels, turtles, and snails as well as fish. Some really have included cats and dogs.

Most scientists say these "rains" are caused by tornado-like whirlwinds. These winds pick up objects and carry them high into the sky. The wind carries them for miles before letting them "rain" down to the ground.

While these winds are the reason for strange rains, two Latin words might be the reason we have the saying "raining cats and dogs." The words are *cata doxas*. The Latin words sound a bit like "cats and dogs." They mean "opposite to experience" or "strange." What could be stranger than a shower of cats and dogs?

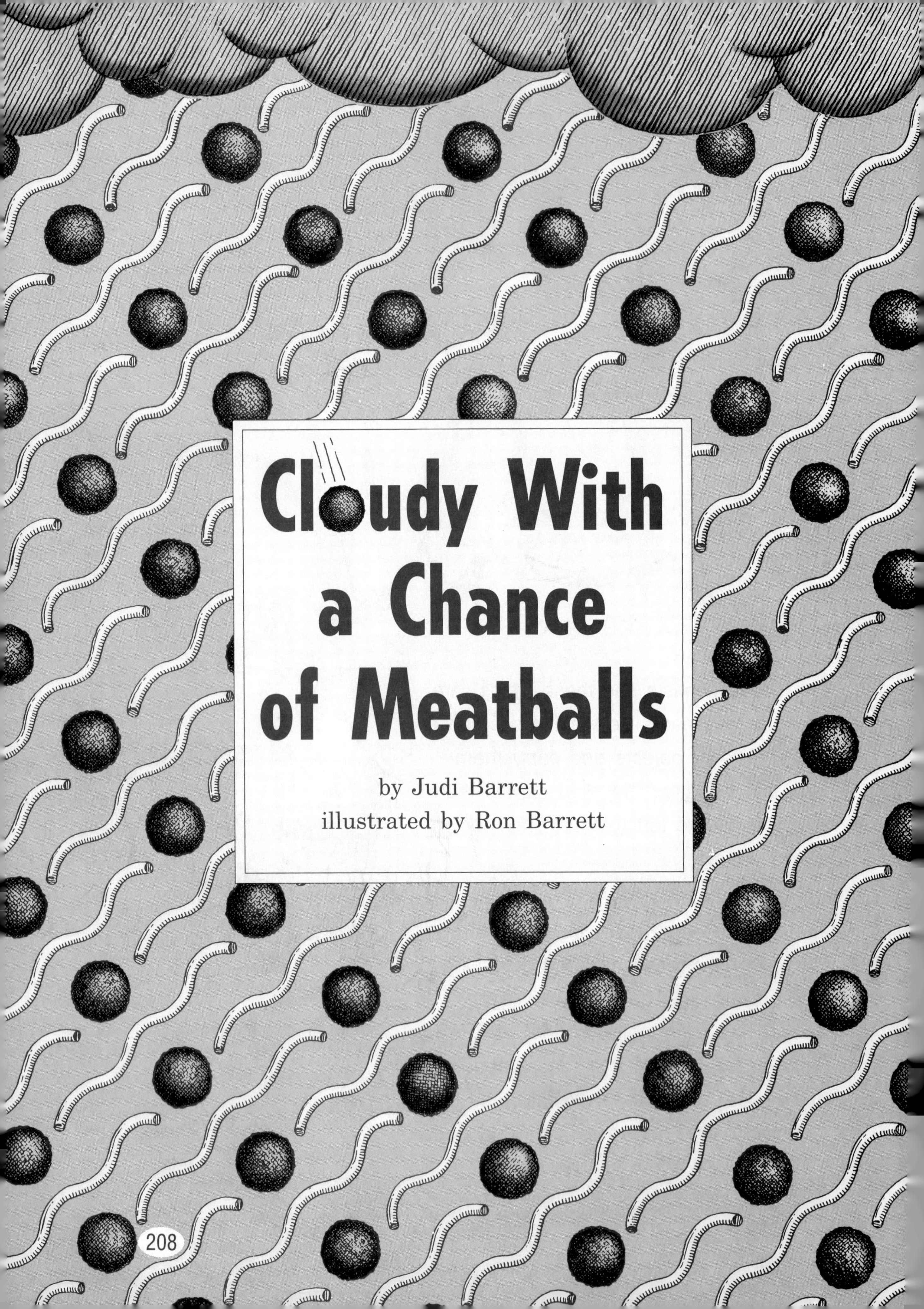

Cloudy With a Chance of Meatballs

by Judi Barrett

illustrated by Ron Barrett

We were all sitting around the big kitchen table. It was Saturday morning. Pancake morning. Mom was squeezing oranges for juice. Henry and I were betting on how many pancakes we each could eat. And Grandpa was doing the flipping.

Seconds later, something flew through the air headed toward
the kitchen ceiling . . .

. . . and landed right on Henry.

After we realized that the flying object was only a pancake, we all laughed, even Grandpa. Breakfast continued quite uneventfully. All the other pancakes landed in the pan. And all of them were eaten, even the one that landed on Henry.

That night, touched off by the pancake incident at breakfast, Grandpa told us the best tall-tale bedtime story he'd ever told.

"Across an ocean, over lots of huge bumpy mountains, across three hot deserts, and one smaller ocean . . .

. . . there lay the tiny town of Chewandswallow.

In most ways, it was very much like any other tiny town. It had a Main Street lined with stores, houses with trees and gardens around them, a schoolhouse, about three hundred people, and some assorted cats and dogs.

But there were no food stores in the town of Chewandswallow. They didn't need any. The sky supplied all the food they could possibly want.

The only thing that was really different about Chewandswallow was its weather. It came three times a day, at breakfast, lunch, and dinner. Everything that everyone ate came from the sky.

215

Whatever the weather served,
that was what they ate.

But it never rained rain. It
never snowed snow. And it never
blew just wind. It rained things
like soup and juice. It snowed
mashed potatoes and green peas.
And sometimes the wind blew
in storms of hamburgers.

216

The people could watch the weather report on television in the morning and they would even hear a prediction for the next day's food.

When the townspeople went outside, they carried their plates, cups, glasses, forks, spoons, knives, and napkins with them. That way they would always be prepared for any kind of weather.

If there were leftovers, and there usually were, the people took them home and put them in their refrigerators in case they got hungry between meals.

The menu varied.

By the time they woke up in the morning, breakfast was coming down.

After a brief shower of orange juice, low clouds of sunny-side-up eggs moved in followed by pieces of toast.

Butter and jelly sprinkled down for the toast. And most of the time it rained milk afterwards.

For lunch one day, frankfurters, already in their rolls, blew in from the northwest at about five miles an hour.

There were mustard clouds nearby. Then the wind shifted to the east and brought in baked beans.

A drizzle of soda finished off the meal.

Dinner one night consisted of lamb chops, becoming heavy at times, with occasional ketchup. Periods of peas and baked potatoes were followed by gradual clearing, with a wonderful Jell-O setting in the west.

The Sanitation Department of Chewandswallow had a rather unusual job for a sanitation department. It had to remove the food that fell on the houses and sidewalks and lawns. The workers cleaned things up after every meal and fed all the dogs and cats. Then they emptied some of it into the surrounding oceans for the fish and turtles and whales to eat. The rest of the food was put back into the earth so that the soil would be richer for the people's flower gardens.

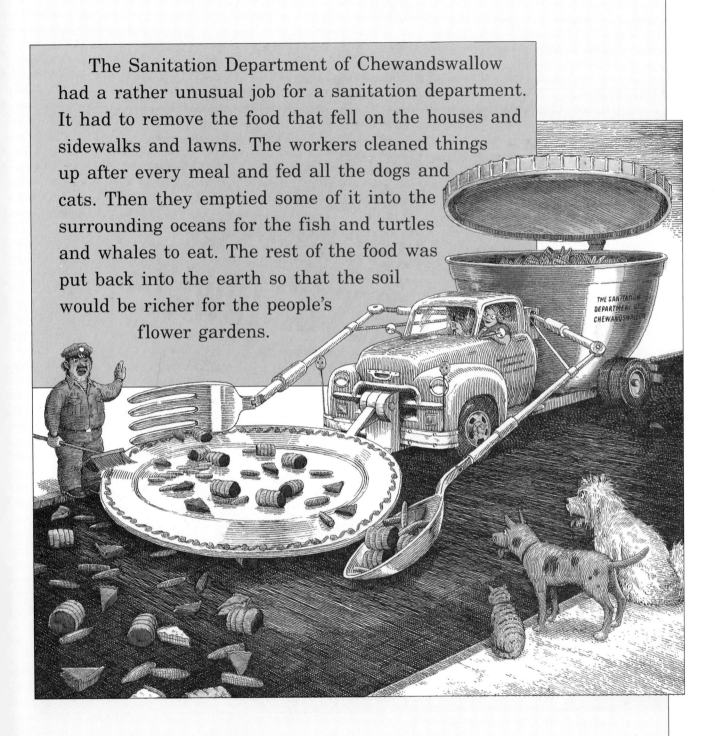

Life for the townspeople was delicious until the weather took a turn for the worse.

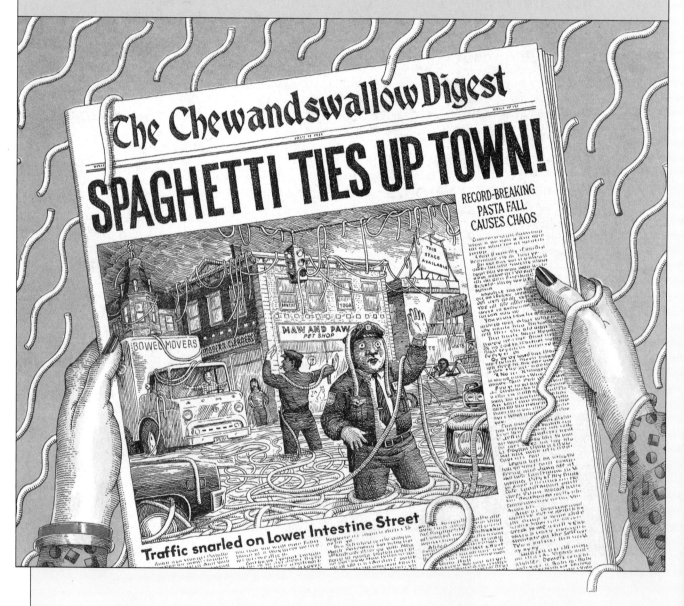

One day there was nothing but Gorgonzola cheese all day long.

The next day there was only broccoli, all overcooked.

And the next day there were Brussels sprouts and peanut butter with mayonnaise.

Another day there was a pea soup fog. No one could see where they were going and they could barely find the rest of the meal that got stuck in the fog.

223

The food was getting larger and larger, and so were the portions. The people were getting frightened. Violent storms blew up frequently. Awful things were happening.

One Tuesday there was a hurricane of bread and rolls all day long and into the night. There were soft rolls and hard rolls, some with seeds and some without. There was white bread and rye and whole wheat toast. Most of it was larger than they had ever seen bread and rolls before. It was a terrible day. Everyone had to stay indoors. Roofs were damaged, and the Sanitation Department was beside itself. The mess took the workers four days to clean up, and the sea was full of floating rolls.

To help out, the people piled up as much bread as they could in their backyards. The birds picked at it a bit, but it just stayed there and got staler and staler.

There was a storm of pancakes one morning and a downpour of maple syrup that nearly flooded the town. A huge pancake covered the school. No one could get it off because of its weight, so they had to close the school.

Lunch one day brought fifteen-inch drifts of cream cheese and jelly sandwiches. Everyone ate themselves sick and the day ended with a stomachache.

There was an awful salt and pepper wind accompanied by an even worse tomato tornado. People were sneezing themselves silly and running to avoid the tomatoes. The town was a mess. There were seeds and pulp everywhere.

The Sanitation Department gave up. The job was too big.

Everyone feared for their lives. They couldn't go outside most of the time. Many houses had been badly damaged by giant meatballs, stores were boarded up and there was no more school for the children.

So a decision was made to abandon the town of Chewandswallow.
It was a matter of survival.
The people glued together the giant pieces of stale bread
sandwich-style with peanut butter...

. . . took the absolute necessities with them, and set sail on their rafts for a new land.

After being afloat for a week, they finally reached a small coastal town, which welcomed them. The bread had held up surprisingly well, well enough for them to build temporary houses for themselves out of it.

The children began school again, and the adults all tried to find places for themselves in the new land. The biggest change they had to make was getting used to buying food at a super-market. They found it odd that the food was kept on shelves, packaged in boxes, cans and bottles. Meat that had to be cooked was kept in large refrigerators. Nothing came down from the sky except rain and snow. The clouds above their heads were not made of fried eggs. No one ever got hit by a hamburger again.

And nobody dared to go back to Chewandswallow to find out what had happened to it. They were too afraid."

Henry and I were awake until the very end of Grandpa's story. I remember his good-night kiss.

The next morning we woke up to see snow falling outside our window.

We ran downstairs for breakfast and ate it a little faster than usual so we could go sledding with Grandpa.

It's funny, but even as we were sliding down the hill we thought we saw a giant pat of butter at the top, and we could almost smell mashed potatoes.

Meet Judi Barrett

Judi Barrett has always had lots of imagination. When she was a child, she loved to make things. She made little people out of peanuts, horses out of pipe cleaners, and dolls out of old quilts.

As an adult, she has used her imagination for writing books, such as *Animals Should Definitely Not Wear Clothing, Benjamin's 365 Birthdays,* and *Cloudy With a Chance of Meatballs.*

Judi Barrett also gets very involved in the art for her books. "I see my books visually while I write them," she says. "The words come along with images of what the book should look like, the feeling it should have."

Meet Ron Barrett

What made Ron Barrett want to draw? It was those silly little characters in the comic books his father used to leave on the table. Ron Barrett remembers all the characters who lived "stacked up in the little boxes on the funny pages."

Ron has kept his sense of humor. Here is what he says about his pictures for *Cloudy With a Chance of Meatballs*: "The book took one year to design and draw. I used a very small pen. Hamburgers and pancakes actually posed for the pictures. I ate my models."

Story Questions & Activities

1 Where did all the food come from in Chewandswallow?

2 What happened when the weather in Chewandswallow took a turn for the worse?

3 Would you like to live in a place like Chewandswallow? Explain.

4 What is this story mainly about?

5 Compare the story that Grandpa tells with the story of Pecos Bill that Cowgirl Pam and Cowboy Sam tell. How are they alike? How are they different?

Write a News Story

Write a humorous news story about the town of Chewandswallow. Give details about what happened to the people in the town.

Create a Comic Strip

Make a comic strip about one of the scenes in "Cloudy With a Chance of Meatballs." Make the panels and then draw the characters in pencil. Use word balloons to tell what happens. After you write in the words, go back and color your comic strip with markers.

Make It Rain

Cut the top half off a plastic soda bottle. Have an adult heat some water until it's almost boiling. Ask them to pour the water into the bottom part of the bottle. Put the top of the bottle back on upside down. Put some ice in the top half of the bottle. Watch what happens to the hot water inside the bottle.

Find Out More

In the Land of Chewandswallow, people watched weather reports to find out what food would be falling out of the sky. What is the weather like in other parts of the world? Choose a place and find out about its weather.

235

Read Signs

Signs are all around us. Some signs give information and other signs advertise things. Signs that advertise things often make use of **propaganda**. Propaganda is information that is often untrue. It often makes something seem more important than it really is.

STOP

BEARSVILLE PUBLIC LIBRARY
Story Time for Tots
FRIDAY AT 3:00

$500 FINE for LITTERING

BEARSVILLE POLICE STATION

Bicycle Safety Talk

WEDNESDAY–7PM

BETSY'S
Home of the Largest and Best Pizza in the World!

TOM'S TOY STORE
Lowest Prices in Town!

Emergency Parking ONLY

AL'S HARDWARE
If you can't buy it here, you can't buy it anywhere!

Use the signs to answer these questions.

1. Which signs are not advertising anything?

2. How much is the fine if you litter in Bearsville?

3. What signs may contain propaganda?

4. What would you have to do to find out if Tom's sign is true?

5. Do the signs at the Public Library and the Police Station use propaganda? Explain.

TEST POWER

Test Tip

Look for clues around the underlined word to help figure out what it means.

DIRECTIONS:

Read the story. Then read each question about the story.

SAMPLE

Tennis

Tennis is one of the most popular games in the world. Players use a racquet to hit a ball back and forth over a net. Tennis can be played with one person on each side of the net. It can also be played with two people on each side of the net. When two people play on each side, it is called doubles tennis.

The goal of the game is to hit the ball to the other side of the net. To score points a player tries to hit the ball so that the other team is not able to hit the ball back. It's great fun to watch or play!

Tennis takes a lot of speed and endurance. A game usually lasts for two to three hours and players run a lot.

Anyone can play tennis, but the best players in the world are strong, fast, and smart.

1 This story is mostly about —

○ what tennis players wear

○ how many can play tennis

○ how to hit a tennis ball

○ how tennis is played

2 In this story, the word endurance means that tennis players must be able to —

○ run for a long time

○ hit the ball over the net

○ play as a team

○ dress differently

237

Stories in Art

A mobile is a special kind of art. Mobiles are made up of hanging parts. When the air moves, the parts move, too.

Look at this mobile. What shapes and colors do you see? What do you think is the main part of the mobile? What title would you give this mobile?

Look closely at the mobile. What do all the moving parts make you think of? Give reasons why you think so.

The Blue Buoy
Artist Unknown

238

Main Idea

Develop a strategy for finding the main idea.

1 **Read the title and the first paragraph.** Do they give you any clues about the article?

2 **Identify who or what** the article is about.

3 **After reading the first paragraph,** what do you think the main idea is?

4 **Read the entire article.** Do the details support the main idea?

5 **State the main idea** in your own words. Is there a similar sentence in the article?

Car Power!

Most cars have gas engines. The exhaust that comes from these engines is one cause of air pollution. Some cars run on energy from the sun. This energy is called solar power. These cars don't burn gas, so they don't cause air pollution.

Every two years, solar cars take part in a special race called the Sunrayce.

Students at Work

Sunrayce cars are made by teams of college students from the United States and Canada.

The cars collect energy from the sun. This energy powers an electric motor that does not cause pollution. The cars also have batteries that store energy. On cloudy days the cars can run on this stored sunlight.

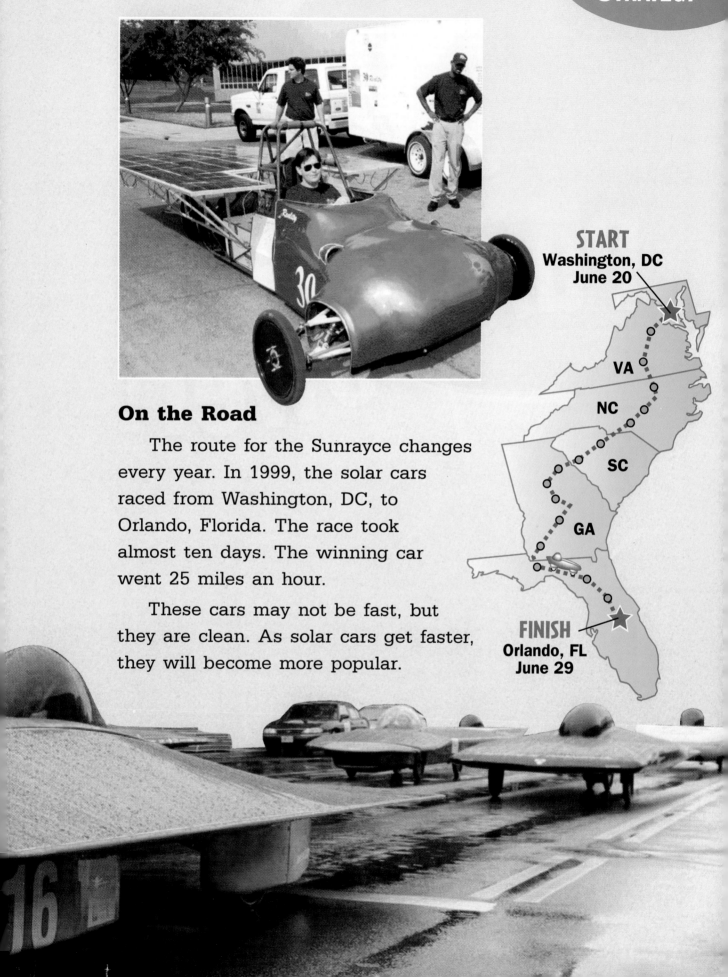

START
Washington, DC
June 20

VA

NC

SC

GA

FINISH
Orlando, FL
June 29

On the Road

The route for the Sunrayce changes every year. In 1999, the solar cars raced from Washington, DC, to Orlando, Florida. The race took almost ten days. The winning car went 25 miles an hour.

These cars may not be fast, but they are clean. As solar cars get faster, they will become more popular.

TIME FOR KIDS

Pure Power!

Scientists are turning the sun and the wind into pollution-free energy.

The Next Wave of Energy

Think of all the ways you used electricity today. Did you turn on a light? Did you watch TV? If you did, you used electric power.

Where does this power come from? In most places, it comes from burning fuels such as gas, coal, and oil. Big factories called power plants burn these fuels to make electricity.

Gas, coal, and oil are fossil fuels. They are formed deep in the Earth from the remains of animals and plants that lived millions of years ago. It takes that long for fossil fuels to form.

Sunshine is frying this egg in a solar cooker.

Someday, cars may run on energy made from the sun. This is a model for a solar-powered car of the future.

241

This California solar "farm" captures energy from the sun. Each of the panels collects sunlight. It will be turned into power.

Most of the world's energy comes from fossil fuels. But burning them gives off dirty gases. This is the world's biggest cause of pollution. So scientists have been looking for cleaner ways to make energy. They've found some answers blowing in the wind and shining in sunlight.

"Sun power and wind power are important for our planet," says Nancy Hazard. She works for a group that studies new kinds of energy.

In Japan, people are building homes with special roof tiles that catch sunlight. The tiles turn the sunlight into electricity. The tiles can make enough electricity for an entire family. About 70,000 of these homes will be built in the next few years.

FIND OUT MORE
Visit our website:
www.mhschool.com/reading

242

Clean as a Breeze

Whirling windmills have been used for energy in countries such as the Netherlands for hundreds of years. Today, windmills are popping up all over the U.S., Europe, and Asia. The modern windmills have lightweight blades that can catch more wind than ever before. They turn the wind into electricity.

One day, we will run out of coal and oil. But we will never run out of the energy we can get from the sun and the wind. Nancy Hazard says, "Energy from the sun and the wind is the key to the future."

LEFT: FPG; RIGHT: PICTOR

The shiny panels on this power plant help turn sunlight into useful energy.

Whirling windmills produce power at this windmill "farm" in California.

DID YOU KNOW?
ELECTRIC FACTS

☀ The sun will burn out in 5 billion years! (So you still have to do your homework!)

✳ The largest wind farm in the world is in Altamont Pass, California. It has 6,500 windmills!

✳ The wind that blows through North Dakota, South Dakota, and Texas could make enough electricity to power the entire U.S.

Based on an article in *TIME FOR KIDS*.

Story Questions & Activities

1. What are two examples of fuels that we burn to make electricity?

2. What are two cleaner sources of energy that the article talks about?

3. Why are scientists looking for new ways to make electricity? Explain.

4. What is the main idea of this selection?

5. If Marcy from "City Green" knew what you know about producing wind energy, what might her next community project be?

Write an Essay

Write an essay that discusses cleaner energy sources. Give three good reasons why using sun or wind power instead of gas, oil, or coal might be a good idea.

Study a Dinosaur

Scientists study fossils to learn about dinosaurs. Make a fact card about your favorite dinosaur. Include where it was found, what types of food it ate, and the period in which it lived. Then draw a picture showing your favorite dinosaur in its habitat.

Make Sun Tea

Use solar energy to make "sun tea." Fill a clean glass jar with bottled water, add tea bags, screw the lid on, and place it next to a sunny window. Record how long it takes for the sun to warm up the water and make the tea.

Find Out More

What kinds of things is solar energy used for? Is it used to heat houses? Can the sun power a car? Find out more by looking in a science book or encyclopedia. Share your findings with the class.

Read an Ad

Advertisements are written to sell products. They first get people interested in a product by saying what it does. Then they make it seem as if people really need the product.

Breeze Headband

~ **Cool down with the new Breeze Headband.**

~ **This unique headband has two fans to keep the heat off! The fans are powered by solar panels.**

~ **The longer you stand in the sun, the cooler you will be! No batteries needed, just the pure power of the sun. It's better than air-conditioning.**

~ **And it's so great looking you'll want to wear it all the time!**

Use the ad to answer these questions.

1 What is a Breeze Headband?

2 Why is the picture an important part of the ad?

3 Do you think everything the ad says is true? Explain.

4 Why do you think the ad says that "you'll want to wear it all the time"?

5 Do you think this ad will make people want to buy the Breeze Headband? Explain.

246

TEST POWER

Test Tip

Remember to read each answer choice before you pick the best one.

DIRECTIONS:

Read the story. Then read each question about the story.

SAMPLE

Eva's Adventures

By the time Eva was eight years old, she had lived in three countries. Her father was asked to move often for his job. Eva did not mind because she looked forward to learning things in each new place.

Eva was very good with words. She had learned to speak three languages. Her favorite language was German because her mom knew it, too. They often had long conversations.

One day Eva said, "Dad, I wish we could live in every country so I could learn every language."

"Eva," her father answered, "I am very proud of you."

1 What is this story mostly about?

○ Eva's father had a good job.

○ Eva looked forward to living in new places.

○ Eva's mother could speak German.

○ Eva liked German best.

2 Which of these is a FACT in this story?

○ Eva spoke German with her mother.

○ Moving to a new place is fun.

○ It is cold in Germany.

○ Eva's parents work very hard.

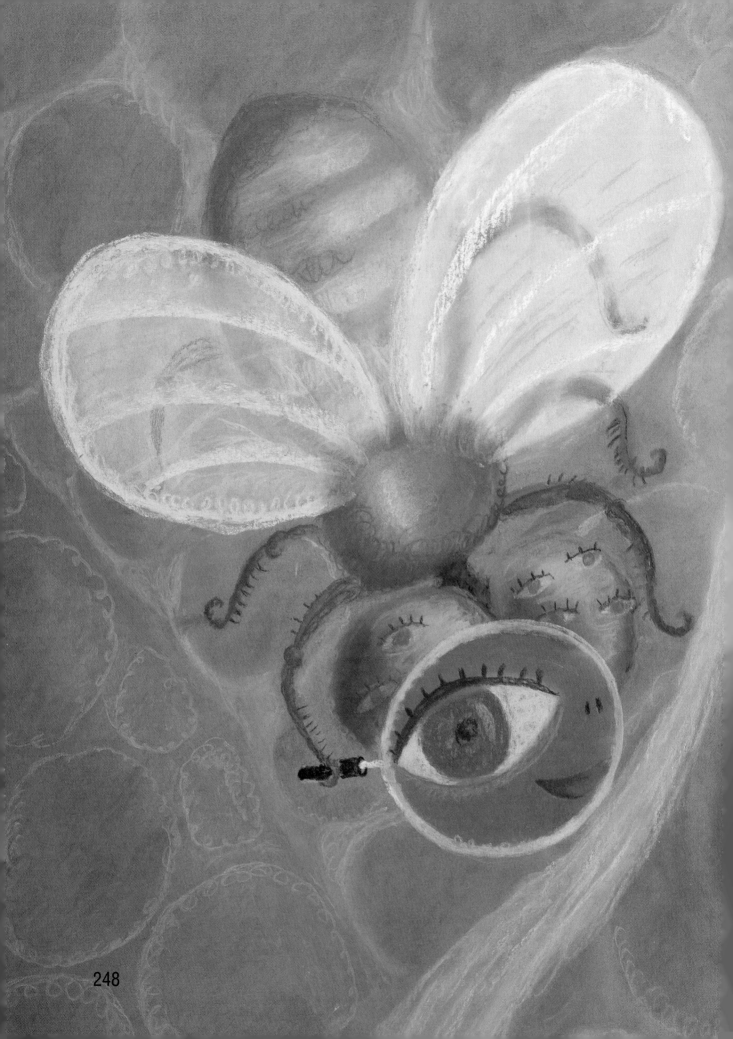

A Fly and a Flea in a Flue

A fly and a flea in a flue
Were imprisoned, so what could they do?
   Said the fly, "Let us flee!"
   "Let us fly!" said the flea,
So they flew through a flaw in the flue.

by P. L. Mannock

Turning Points

Dreams

Hold fast to dreams
For if dreams die
Life is a broken-winged bird
That cannot fly.

Hold fast to dreams
For when dreams go
Life is a barren field
Frozen with snow.

by Langston Hughes

Stories in Art

This painting shows part of a story. By looking at the clues the artist has given us, we can figure out what is happening.

Look at the painting. What can you tell about it? Why is the man holding his hand up toward the sky? Why is everyone else looking at him? What do you think will happen next?

If this painting suddenly came to life, what sounds might you hear?

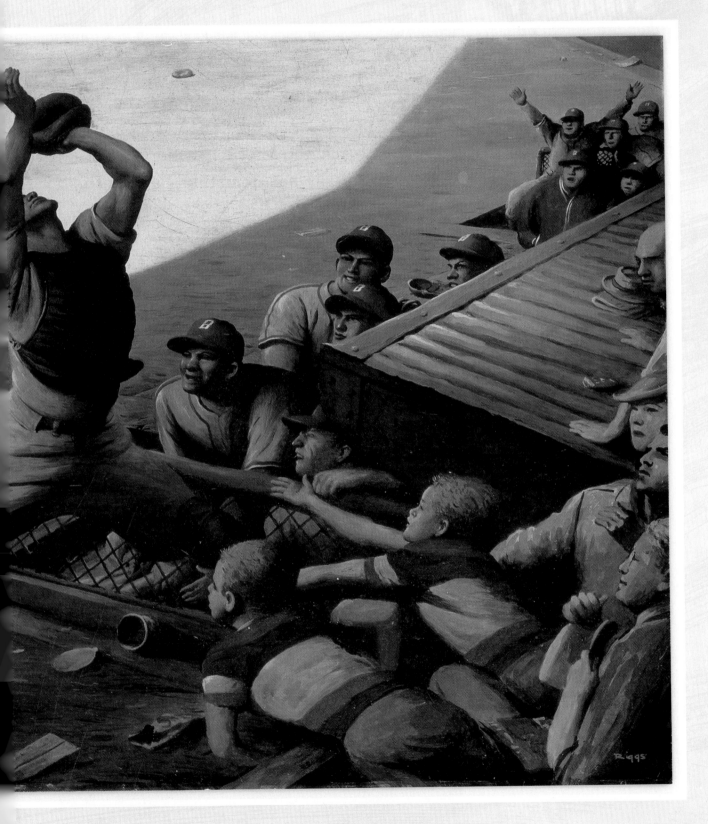

Catcher on the Line by Robert Riggs

NEW GAME

Make Inferences

Develop a strategy for making inferences.

1 **What is the story about?** When does it take place?

2 **Note story details.** What can you tell about the characters from their actions and words?

3 **Look at the chart.** What information does it add to the story?

4 **Make an inference.** Did Betsy's father enjoy the baseball game?

It was the first game of the 1947 season. The Kenosha Comets were playing the South Bend Blue Sox. Betsy sat near first base with her mom and dad.

Last summer, when Dad was away in the army, Betsy and Mom had gone to every game. Now Dad was home, and he was about to see his first All-American Girls baseball game.

The players came out of their dugouts. "Wow!" said Dad. "These girls look like they are ready for anything!"

IN TOWN

The game started slowly. The first batter walked. The next one struck out. Betsy's dad looked worried. "I want these teams to look good," he said. And he let out a cheer.

The third batter hit a ground ball. The Comets' shortstop scooped it up and tossed it to second for a forced out. The second baseman threw the ball to first for a double play. Betsy's dad leaned forward in his seat.

The Comets finally went on to win the game 5 to 3!

As they got up to leave, Betsy's dad said, "When's the next game?"

All-American Girls Professional Baseball League

FORT WAYNE DAISIES,
Fort Wayne, Indiana

GRAND RAPIDS CHICKS,
Grand Rapids, Michigan

KENOSHA COMETS,
Kenosha, Wisconsin

MUSKEGON LASSIES,
Muskegon, Michigan

PEORIA REDWINGS,
Peoria, Illinois

RACINE BELLES,
Racine, Wisconsin

ROCKFORD PEACHES,
Rockford, Illinois

SOUTH BEND BLUE SOX,
South Bend, Indiana

Meet Gavin Curtis

Gavin Curtis grew up in a New York City public housing project. There he spent hours in the corner of his living room writing and illustrating stories about superheroes.

Curtis studied illustration, animation, and film at the School of Visual Arts in New York City. Then, when he was 22 years old, he started writing and illustrating for Marvel Comics. That same year, he also wrote and illustrated his first book, *Grandma's Baseball.*

About his book, *The Bat Boy and His Violin,* Curtis says, "If there is a lesson readers and future artists can learn from Reginald's tale, it is to follow your dreams."

Meet E.B. Lewis

When E.B. Lewis was in the third grade, he was showing a talent for art. By the time he was in the seventh grade, Lewis was in art school. Today Lewis's work is displayed in art galleries throughout the United States.

When Lewis illustrates a book, he often uses real people as models. For *The Bat Boy and His Violin,* he modeled Reginald after his own son Joshua.

The Bat Boy and His Violin

WRITTEN BY
Gavin Curtis

ILLUSTRATED BY
E. B. Lewis

I sashay my bow across the violin strings the way a mosquito skims a summer pond. With hardly any mistakes, Tchaikovsky fills the living room of our house on Tyler Road. When the back door slams and metal cleats stomp onto the kitchen floor, I know Papa is home.

"Is—Reginald—at—it—again?" he shouts between notes.

"Hush up," Mama says, "I just love this one."

"Cooped up inside all the time, it's a wonder that boy don't sprout mushrooms."

I try to play louder than Papa's voice by sawing the music hard. He sometimes comes home in a bad mood because he's the manager of the Dukes—the worst team in the Negro National League. So far, the 1948 season has been the toughest yet. Papa's even having trouble booking games the team is likely to lose. He says it's because all his best hitters and fielders are going over to play for white teams, the way Jackie Robinson did last year.

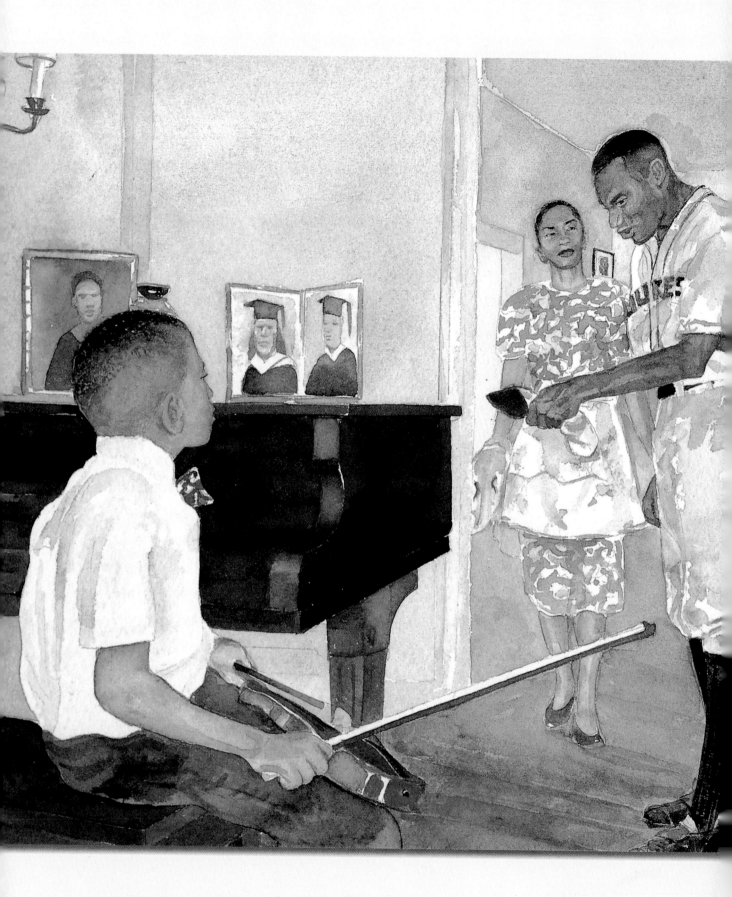

"You know our baby wants to be in a famous orchestra someday," Mama says, following Papa into the living room.

"Well, right now the Dukes could use a bat boy, and I think it'll do Reginald some good to get out the house. We'll get him a uniform and everything."

I stop playing. "What about my practice?" I ask. "Don't you remember I have a recital next month in the basement at church?"

"You can rehearse 'tween innings. Tendin' to bats don't take up no whole lotta time." Papa pretends to swing one at an invisible pitch. "Anyway, you do a good job and I'll let you have your fiddle recital right here."

I smile because our living room is bigger than the church basement. "I prefer to call it a violin," I say.

Papa doesn't hear. He's too busy admiring the trophy cabinet. "Heck," Papa says, "this might even inspire you to become a ball player the way your ol' man was."

The next morning, I ride with Papa and the Dukes to Cleveland on the team's rickety old bus. We get to the field for our game against the Buckeyes, and the bleachers are already packed with their fans.

Mr. Forrest, the shortstop, is the first one up. I want to do a good job, so I bring him six bats to choose from. It's too many, and they roll out of my hands and make Mr. Forrest stumble like he's skating on ice. He lands flat on his backside, making the crowd howl like they've just seen a circus clown performance.

"One at a time, boy!" Papa's face is all crinkled.

Mr. Forrest gets up and misses the ball three times.

Nobody else falls, but the next two outs come quickly. The Dukes take the field, and I notice some bats are scuffed from Mr. Forrest's cleats. I remember the polish I use on my violin, and I buff the bats clean with a towel until they shine. I lean them with the others evenly in a row against the fence, standing beside them ready for when it's the Dukes's turn to bat again—praying nothing more goes wrong.

"Startin' to get the hang of it, ain't ya," Papa says.

"Yep," I say, rocking heel to toe and toe to heel.

Mr. Mosley, the third baseman, tips his cap because I hand him a bat. When he swings at the pitch, the bat slips out of his hand and misses the umpire's head by no more than an inch.

"I'll pass out the bats," Papa says after the umpire has calmed down. Papa grumbles under his breath because the umpire makes him rub dirt on each bat.

"Can I help?" I ask.

"Why don't you relax a spell on the bench. It'll give you a chance to fiddle."

"You mean violin."

"Just keep it low. Lord knows I don't need nothing makin' my headache worse." Papa takes his cap off and uses it to wipe the sweat from his face.

I play *Swan Lake* the way I feel—sad and quiet. But I'm not clumsy with my violin. I'm careful, glancing only one time at the music I know by heart. In the last measure, I pull my bow slowly to hold the final note long.

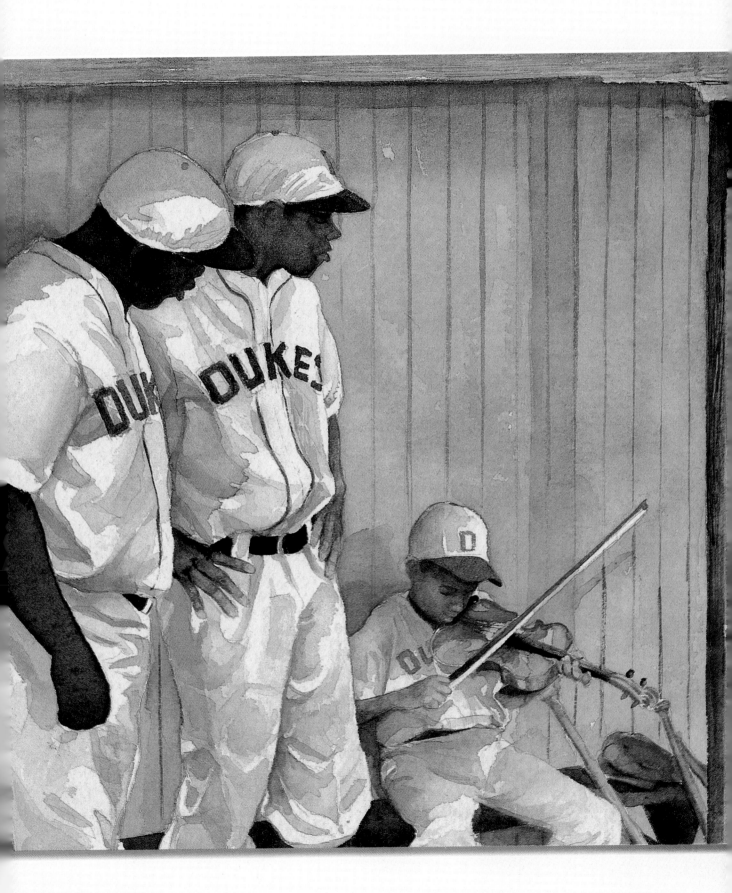

"That sure was somethin' pretty," says Mr. LaRue, the center fielder who is waiting on deck. "Kinda makes the hairs on the back of my neck do a jig."

"Thank you," I say, a little embarrassed that anyone had listened.

"You're up, LaRue," Papa calls. His headache must have disappeared, because a smile crosses his face. "How 'bout doin' a *jig* with that bat and getting a hit?"

As Mr. LaRue steps up to the plate, I start to play again. He lets the first pitch go past him but swings hard on the next.

"RUN!" Papa yells because Mr. LaRue sends the ball toward the outfield.

Before he can reach first base, the ball leaves the park. He takes his time and does a kind of hop around the field while I play until he gets back to home plate.

Mr. Ervin, the catcher, bats next, and I play Mozart—and the same thing happens again. It happens with the left fielder, the second baseman, and the third baseman, too.

I'm bushed by the ninth inning, but the Dukes have beaten the Buckeyes, seven to four. It's the first game they win in months.

"Ain't this a talented boy," Papa says, and massages *my* arm instead of the pitcher's.

Each day, I like being the bat boy more than the last. Papa handles the bats, and he lets me play my violin as much as I want. Besides that, the Dukes have stopped losing. I haven't seen Papa this happy since he was a player.

Three weeks into our winning streak, Papa makes an important announcement. "We got us a game with the Monarchs!"

I'm the only one not cheering, so I ask, "Are they any good?"

"Any good?" he says. "Why, they're the best colored team there is."

"I thought *we* were," I say.

"If we beat them Monarchs, we will be. Folks are sayin' now that baseball's becoming integrated, the Negro Leagues won't be 'round forever. The season's coming to an end, and this might be the Dukes's last chance to make a real mark—make a name for ourselves." Papa lifts me up onto his shoulder. "Good thing we got us a gifted little bat boy."

The night before the big game, Papa can't find a hotel in town that will accept the Dukes. "We don't exactly cotton to coloreds sleepin' in our beds," one white clerk says. "Y'all gonna have to look elsewheres."

"Thank you kindly just the same," Papa says, tipping his cap. "I reckon our bus will do us fine."

We park on a field outside the stadium, and Mr. LaRue grills catfish and corn on the cob. After dinner, fancying their chances of winning a pennant makes the team too jittery to sleep, so I play them a lullaby Mama sometimes hums to me before bed.

"Reginald," Papa says when the sound of snores joins the sound of crickets, "you got a knack. That fool clerk should have heard your pretty fiddlin'."

"*Violining*," I tell Papa before falling asleep on his belly.

The next day, the sun is high and little shade can be found once the game has gone into extra innings. I play my best, but nothing seems to work—at least not for the Dukes. I play Beethoven, and Mr. Forrest and Mr. Mosley both hit balls that seem to fly right back into the pitcher's glove. I play Mozart, and Mr. LaRue is tagged out at home. But when I play Bach with the game tied, two outs and Papa very nervous, Mr. O'Neil from the Monarchs knocks a high, curling wallop into deep left field.

I stop playing just in time to see the ball easily clear the fence. The Dukes lose, eighteen to seventeen.

The team congratulates the Monarchs and heads for the showers. No one says anything when they walk past me. Papa looks sad as he gathers up the equipment. I want to help him, but I go straight to the bus instead, wondering if the church basement is still available for my recital.

"Son," Papa finally says on the quiet ride home, "play somethin' happy." He takes the violin down from the baggage rack and hands it to me. "We could all use a little cheerin' up."

"I...I was afraid you wouldn't like my music anymore." I twist the pegs and make sure it's tuned.

"Of course I still like your music," Papa sits in the seat and puts me on his lap. "It sure helped us get a lot further than I thought we could without our best players. Shoot, when I shut my big mouth and listened, I loved what I heard. I love you, though, most of all. Win or lose—Negro Leagues or not—ain't no ball game ever gonna change that."

"I love you, too, Papa." I hug him and then play the "Minute Waltz" over and over again.

A week later, baseball season is over, and at last I perform my recital. The only sound heard through our house on Tyler Road is the softness of a Schubert sonata—with no mistakes. Mama, Papa, the Dukes and their wives fill the first four rows of our crowded living room.

"You folks must be right proud of Reginald," I hear Mr. LaRue whisper. "He sure plays a powerful fiddle."

Papa smiles and puts his arm around Mama. "Sure does," he says, "'cept, we prefer to call it a *violin*."

Story Questions & Activities

1 What did Papa call Reginald's violin in the beginning of the story?

2 Why did Reginald become the bat boy for the Dukes?

3 At the end of the story, how did Papa feel about Reginald playing the violin?

4 What is this story mainly about?

5 If Moses and Reginald met each other, what might they talk about?

Write a Sequel

Write a sequel to "The Bat Boy and His Violin." What do you think will happen next to Reginald and his father? Use some dialogue to make your story come alive.

Listen to Classical Music

Reginald loves to play classical music. At the library, look for recordings by one of the composers mentioned in the selection, such as Mozart. Listen to the recording and draw pictures that you think go with the music.

Sports

What sport do you especially enjoy playing or watching? With a partner, interview each other about your favorite sports. Share some facts about your sport and tell why you enjoy following or participating in it.

Find Out More

Did you know that there is a Negro League Museum in Kansas City, Missouri? Find out what you can see there. Think of five questions you'd like to know about the Negro Leagues. Then write a class letter to the museum.

279

Use the Library

After reading about Reginald, you might want to learn more about classical music or the Negro Leagues. You can find books, magazines, newspapers, and videos at the **library**. At the **circulation desk**, you can check out a book, magazine, or video to take home.

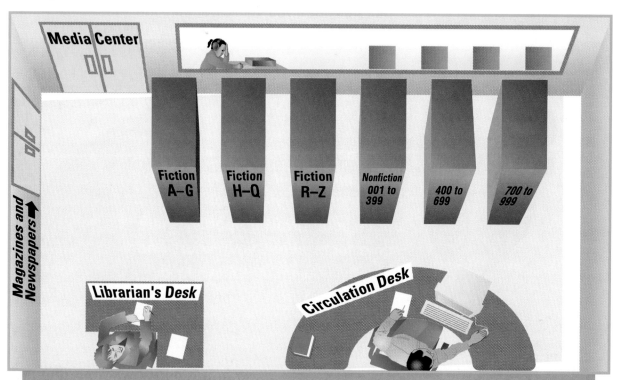

Media Center

Magazines and Newspapers

Fiction A–G

Fiction H–Q

Fiction R–Z

Nonfiction 001 to 399

400 to 699

700 to 999

Librarian's *Desk*

Circulation Desk

Use the diagram to answer these questions.

1. Which part of the library would you go to if you wanted to check out a book?

2. In which section would you find a book on baseball?

3. In which section would you find a recording by Mozart?

4. In which section would you find a magazine about music?

5. In which sections of the library would you enjoy browsing? Explain.

TEST POWER

Test *Tip*

A FACT is something that is true, is in the story, and is not an opinion.

DIRECTIONS:

Read the story. Then read each question about the story.

SAMPLE

Police Officers

Everyone is very glad there are police officers. They are the men and women who help keep everyone safe in your city or town.

The police in your area work as a team and help people in need. They go through special training so that they will know how to solve problems as quickly as possible.

Police officers carry special radios so that they can talk to the other officers. When they see someone in trouble, they can call more officers to come and help.

Being a police officer is rewarding work. The police officers know that you look to them for safety and guidance. That's what their job is all about!

1 The story says people think that police officers—

○ should work harder

○ keep people safe

○ are not very fast

○ look silly in their uniforms

2 In this story, which is NOT a fact about police officers?

○ They know you look to them for safety.

○ They work alone.

○ They think being a police officer is rewarding.

○ They keep everyone safe.

Stories in Art

Two Quarry Fish by Karl Ciesluk, 1993

Some photographs can surprise us. They make us see things in new and different ways.

~~~~~

Look at the photograph. What do you see? How do you think the rocks got that way? Do you think the photographer wanted people to see the rocks reflected in the water? Why?

~~~~~

Look again at the photograph. How is it both the same as and different from a painting?

The **Ant** and

Draw Conclusions

Develop a strategy for drawing conclusions.

① **Read the title.** What do you expect the story to be about?

② **Look at the pictures.** How do they help you understand the story?

③ **Think about the characters.** How would you describe them?

④ **Think about what you know** about fables. What usually happens in a fable?

⑤ **Draw a conclusion.** What lesson does the story teach?

It was a perfect summer day, and Grasshopper was enjoying every minute of it. She hopped around the garden. She chirped. She sang. She was having a wonderful time.

While Grasshopper enjoyed the day, Ant was working. Grasshopper watched him as he struggled to drag a seed along the ground.

"What are you doing?" she asked. "Where are you going with that seed?"

"I'm going to store it in my nest," said Ant.

"Why?" said Grasshopper. "The garden is full of good things to eat."

"Now it is," said Ant. "But it won't be in the winter. So I'm gathering food."

the Grasshopper

"Winter is a long way off," said Grasshopper. "I'm not going to waste this perfectly beautiful day worrying about it."

"It's your choice," said Ant. "But you'll be sorry."

So Ant kept on working, and Grasshopper kept on enjoying herself. She sang and chirped and hopped and danced all through the summer and the fall.

But when winter came, Grasshopper saw how foolish she had been. Ant, who had worked and planned, had plenty of food. But Grasshopper had none.

MEET *Chris Van Allsburg*

If you saw ants in your kitchen, what would you think? If you are like a lot of people, you might think "How disgusting!" or "How interesting!" or "How cute!" However, when Chris Van Allsburg saw two ants in his kitchen, he thought: "If I were an ant looking out from an electrical socket, the long slits in which the light poured in would look like 15-foot doorways hung in space." That thought gave Chris Van Allsburg the idea for *Two Bad Ants*.

Chris Van Allsburg, with some of the sculptures he has created

Chris Van Allsburg's talent for looking at the world in unusual ways has won him the highest award for children's picture books in the United States—the Caldecott Medal. He won it not just once, but twice: for *Jumanji* in 1982 and for *The Polar Express* in 1986.

Van Allsburg's way of looking at the world has also won him many fans. One fan wrote: "I love the books you write. I am so glad you are weird because I am very weird. I think you are weird but great."

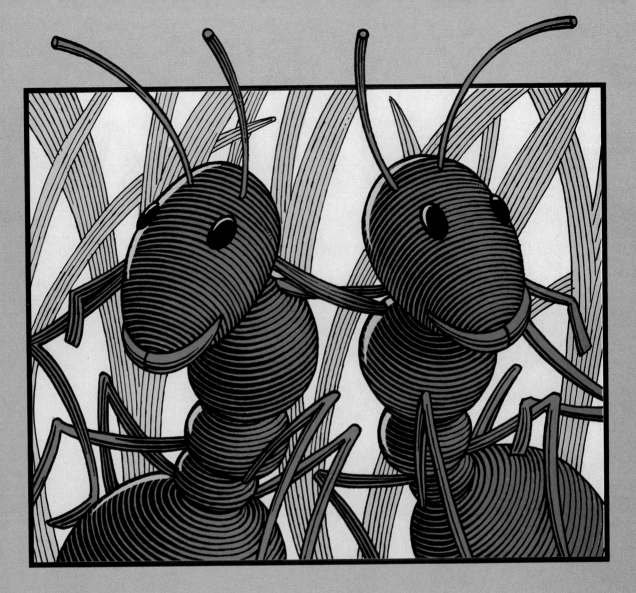

TWO
BAD
ANTS

CHRIS VAN ALLSBURG

The news traveled swiftly through the tunnels
of the ant world. A scout had returned with a
remarkable discovery—a beautiful sparkling
crystal. When the scout presented the crystal to
the ant queen she took a small bite, then quickly
ate the entire thing.

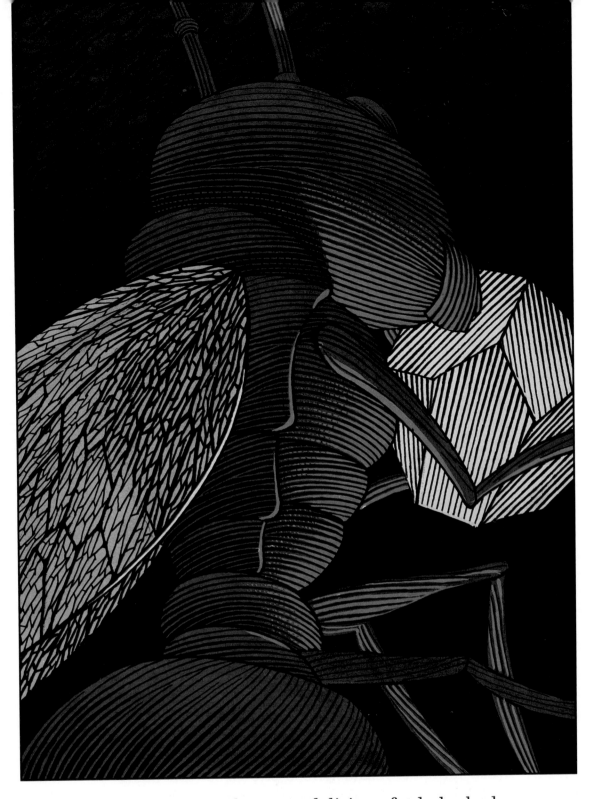

She deemed it the most delicious food she had
ever tasted. Nothing could make her happier than
to have more, much more. The ants understood.
They were eager to gather more crystals because
the queen was the mother of them all. Her
happiness made the whole ant nest a happy place.

It was late in the day when they departed.
Long shadows stretched over the entrance to the
ant kingdom. One by one the insects climbed out,
following the scout, who had made it clear—there
were many crystals where the first had been
found, but the journey was long and dangerous.

They marched into the woods that surrounded
their underground home. Dusk turned to twilight,
twilight to night. The path they followed twisted
and turned, every bend leading them deeper into
the dark forest.

288

More than once the line of ants stopped and
anxiously listened for the sounds of hungry
spiders. But all they heard was the call of crickets
echoing through the woods like distant thunder.

Dew formed on the leaves above. Without
warning, huge cold drops fell on the marching
ants. A firefly passed overhead that, for an
instant, lit up the woods with a blinding flash of
blue-green light.

At the edge of the forest stood a mountain. The ants looked up and could not see its peak. It seemed to reach right to the heavens. But they did not stop. Up the side they climbed, higher and higher.

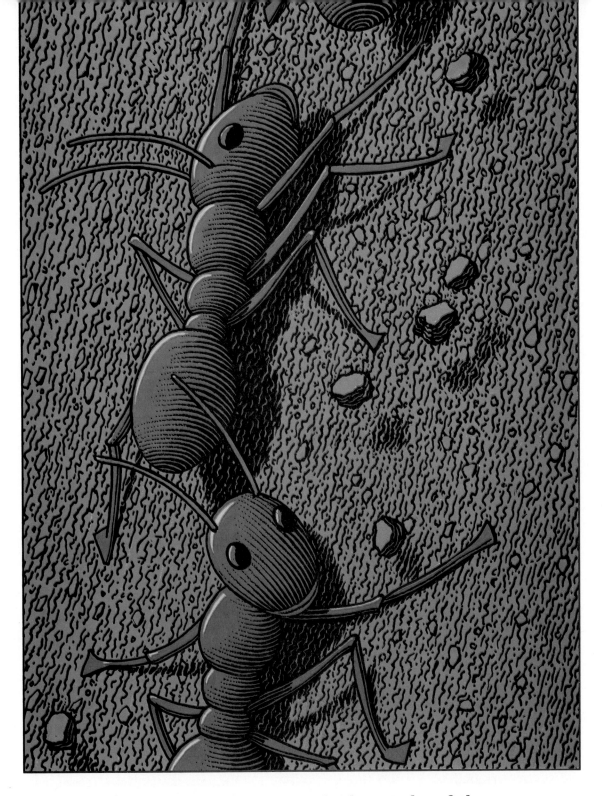

The wind whistled through the cracks of the
mountain's face. The ants could feel its force bending
their delicate antennae. Their legs grew weak as
they struggled upward. At last they reached a ledge
and crawled through a narrow tunnel.

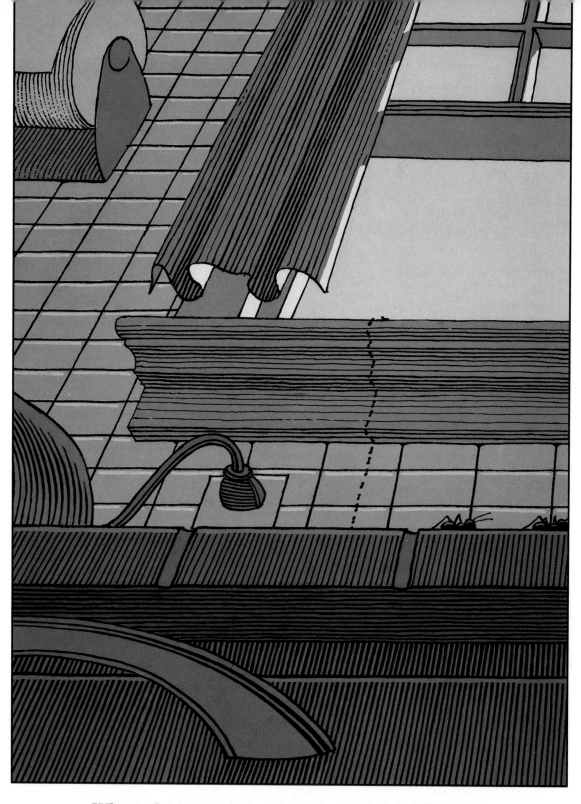

When the ants came out of the tunnel they
found themselves in a strange world. Smells they
had known all their lives, smells of dirt and grass
and rotting plants, had vanished. There was no
more wind and, most puzzling of all, it seemed
that the sky was gone.

They crossed smooth shiny surfaces, then
followed the scout up a glassy, curved wall. They
had reached their goal. From the top of the wall
they looked below to a sea of crystals. One by one
the ants climbed down into the sparkling treasure.

Quickly they each chose a crystal, then turned
to start the journey home. There was something
about this unnatural place that made the ants
nervous. In fact they left in such a hurry that
none of them noticed the two small ants who
stayed behind.

"Why go back?" one asked the other. "This
place may not feel like home, but look at all these
crystals." "You're right," said the other, "we can
stay here and eat this tasty treasure every day,
forever." So the two ants ate crystal after crystal
until they were too full to move, and fell asleep.

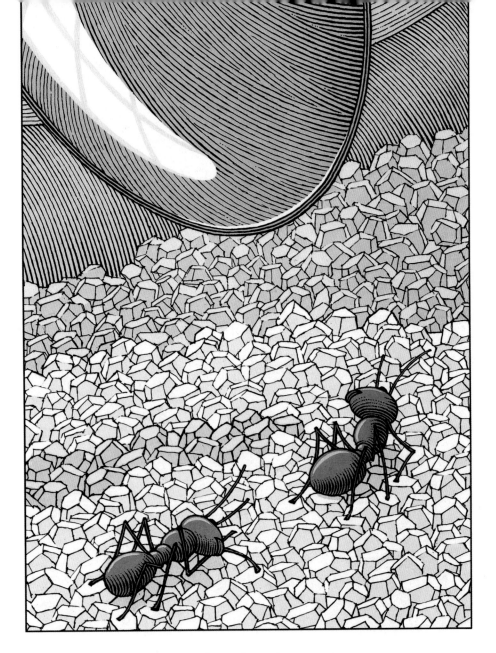

Daylight came. The sleeping ants were unaware of changes taking place in their new found home. A giant silver scoop hovered above them, then plunged deep into the crystals. It shoveled up both ants and crystals and carried them high into the air.

The ants were wide awake when the scoop turned, dropping them from a frightening height. They tumbled through space in a shower of crystals and fell into a boiling brown lake.

Then the giant scoop stirred violently back and forth. Crushing waves fell over the ants. They paddled hard to keep their tiny heads above water. But the scoop kept spinning the hot brown liquid.

Around and around it went, creating a whirlpool that sucked the ants deeper and deeper. They both held their breath and finally bobbed to the surface, gasping for air and spitting mouthfuls of the terrible, bitter water.

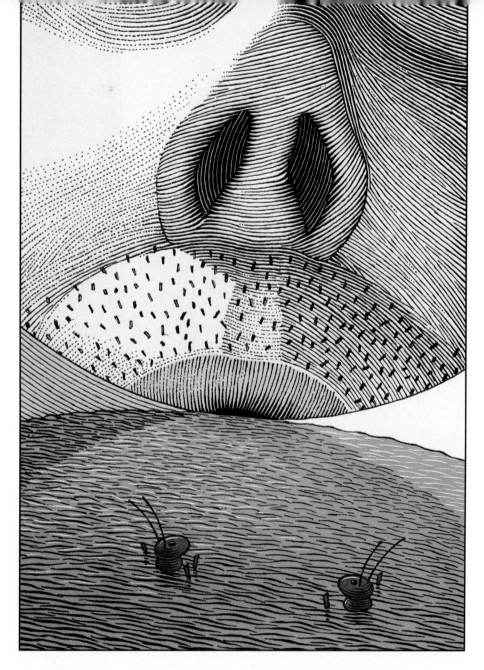

Then the lake tilted and began to empty into a cave. The ants could hear the rushing water and felt themselves pulled toward the pitch black hole. Suddenly the cave disappeared and the lake became calm. The ants swam to the shore and found that the lake had steep sides.

They hurried down the walls that held back the lake. The frightened insects looked for a place to hide, worried that the giant scoop might shovel them up again. Close by they found a huge round disk with holes that could neatly hide them.

But as soon as they had climbed inside, their
hiding place was lifted, tilted, and lowered into a
dark space. When the ants climbed out of the
holes they were surrounded by a strange red glow.
It seemed to them that every second the
temperature was rising.

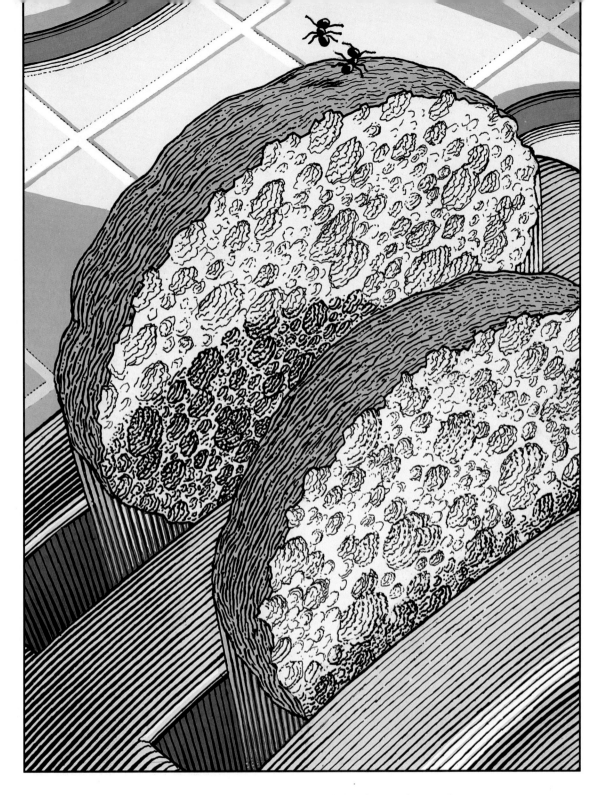

It soon became so unbearably hot that they
thought they would soon be cooked. But suddenly
the disk they were standing on rocketed upward
and the two hot ants went flying through the air.

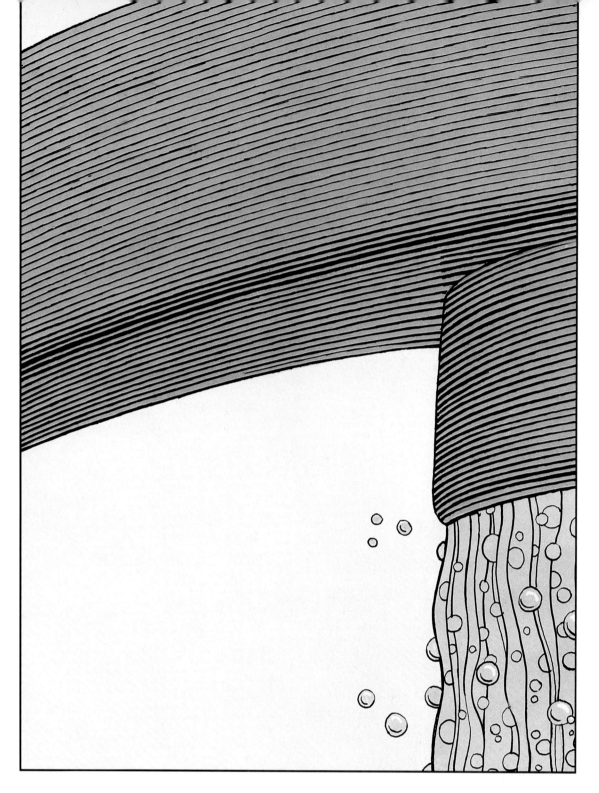

They landed near what seemed to be a
fountain—a waterfall pouring from a silver tube.
Both ants had a powerful thirst and longed to dip
their feverish heads into the refreshing water.
They quickly climbed along the tube.

As they got closer to the rushing water the
ants felt a cool spray. They tightly gripped the
shiny surface of the fountain and slowly leaned
their heads into the falling stream. But the force
of the water was much too strong.

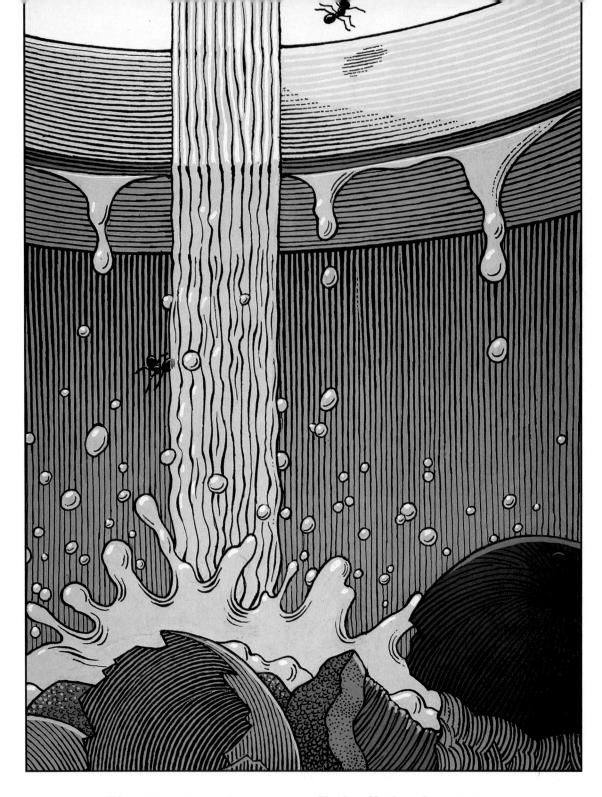

The tiny insects were pulled off the fountain
and plunged down into a wet, dark chamber. They
landed on half-eaten fruit and other soggy things.
Suddenly the air was filled with loud, frightening
sounds. The chamber began to spin.

The ants were caught in a whirling storm of shredded food and stinging rain. Then, just as quickly as it had started, the noise and spinning stopped. Bruised and dizzy, the ants climbed out of the chamber.

In daylight once again, they raced through puddles and up a smooth metal wall. In the distance they saw something comforting—two long, narrow holes that reminded them of the warmth and safety of their old underground home. They climbed up into the dark openings.

But there was no safety inside these holes. A strange force passed through the wet ants. They were stunned senseless and blown out of the holes like bullets from a gun. When they landed the tiny insects were too exhausted to go on. They crawled into a dark corner and fell fast asleep.

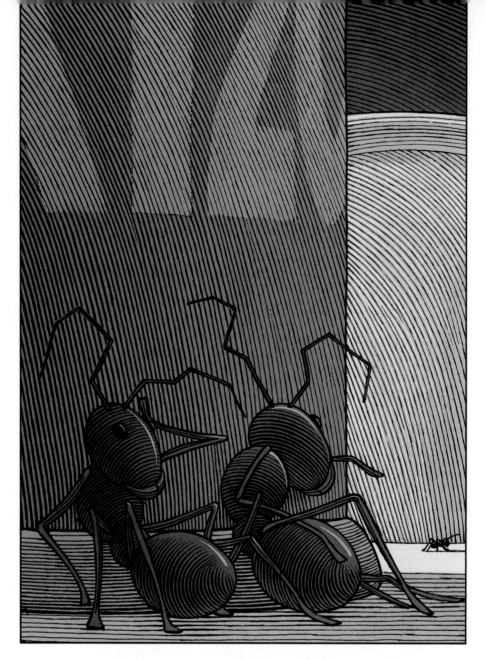

Night had returned when the battered ants awoke to a familiar sound—the footsteps of their fellow insects returning for more crystals. The two ants slipped quietly to the end of the line. They climbed the glassy wall and once again stood amid the treasure. But this time they each chose a single crystal and followed their friends home.

Standing at the edge of their ant hole, the
two ants listened to the joyful sounds that came
from below. They knew how grateful their
mother queen would be when they gave her
their crystals. At that moment, the two ants felt
happier than they'd ever felt before. This was
their home, this was their family. This was
where they were meant to be.

Story Questions & Activities

1. Why did the two ants decide to stay behind?

2. What happened to the ants when they woke up in the morning?

3. What do you think the two ants learned from their experiences?

4. What is this story mostly about?

5. Imagine that the two bad ants went to visit the Land of Opt. What kinds of adventures might they have there?

Write a Dialogue

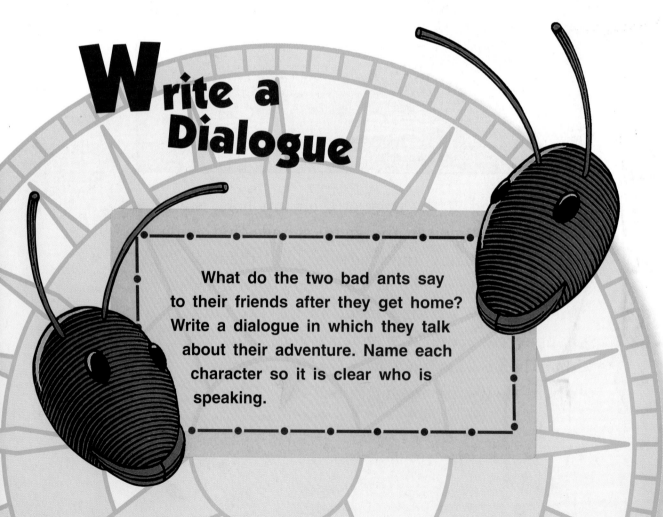

What do the two bad ants say to their friends after they get home? Write a dialogue in which they talk about their adventure. Name each character so it is clear who is speaking.

Make a Papier-mâché Ant

Make a papier-mâché model of an ant. Form the body of the ant using balloons. In a bowl, mix flour and water. Coat strips of newspaper with the mixture and place them on the balloons. Paint when dry.

Create an Insect Collage

Look for pictures of insects in old magazines, and cut out your favorite images. Also draw pictures of insects yourself. Use the photos and drawings to create an insect collage.

Find Out More

Find out more about ants. Do ant communities really have a queen? What do the workers do? How do ants find and store food? Get all the ant-swers!

STUDY SKILLS

Do an Author and Title Search

To do an electronic author search, type in the name of the author—Chris Van Allsburg. You will see a list of the books by the author that your library has, as on the screen below. To do an electronic title search, type in the title of a book. You will see an alphabetical list of book titles.

Author and Title	Call Number	© Date
1. Van Allsburg, Chris Jumanji	J Fic V	1981
2. Van Allsburg, Chris Just a Dream	J Pic V	1990
3. Van Allsburg, Chris The Polar Express	J Fic V	1985
4. Van Allsburg, Chris The Sweetest Fig	J Pic V	1993
4 items	[B] = go back	[R] = go to next screen

Use the results of the search to answer the questions.

1 How many items came up in the search?

2 Which of the books on the screen was published in 1990?

3 *J* stands for the Juvenile section of the library. How many of the books listed would be found there?

4 *Pic* stands for *Picture Book* and *Fic* stands for *Fiction*. What do you think the *V* stands for?

5 Why would it be interesting to read more stories by Chris Van Allsburg?

TEST POWER

Test Tip
Look for clues around the underlined word to help figure out what it means.

DIRECTIONS:
Read the story. Then read each question about the story.

SAMPLE

Did Turtle Win the Race?

One day the turtle <u>crawled</u> past the rabbit at his usual slow pace. He overheard the rabbit say that he was the fastest creature on four legs. The turtle said, "I think I can beat you in a race."

The rabbit fell over laughing and said, "If you really think so, then we must race."

They lined up at a tree, and the owl said "Go!"

The rabbit hopped ahead as fast as he could. The turtle went slowly. After a few minutes, the rabbit was far ahead but very tired. He decided to take a nap. At the same time, the turtle kept at his usual pace. He was not tired at all. The turtle crawled past the sleeping rabbit and kept going to the finish line. The turtle won the race!

1 You know that story is make-believe because –

○ squirrels can run

○ turtles are slow

○ rabbits are fast

○ animals cannot talk

2 The word <u>crawled</u> in this story means –

○ moved slowly

○ ran quickly

○ lay down

○ rolled over

311

Stories in Art

An Intense Study by Horatio Henry Couldery

The parts of a painting can be like pieces of a puzzle. Each one gives a little information. When all the parts are put together, they tell a story.

Look at this painting. What can you tell about the kittens? What story do you think the artist wants to tell? What do you think might happen next? Give reasons why you think so.

Close your eyes. What do you remember about the painting? Why?

Make Inferences

Develop a strategy for making inferences.

1 **Read the title** and first paragraph. What do you think the article will be about?

2 **Think about what you know.** What do you already know about the topic?

3 **Look at the details.** What facts and examples does the article give?

4 **Study the pictures.** What information do they give you about the subject?

5 **Make an inference.** How do you think Koko's trainers feel about her? How do you know?

WHAT DO YOU SAY, KOKO?

Koko the gorilla was born in 1971. When she was one year old, her trainer began to teach her American sign language. Koko proved to be a good student. She now uses more than 1,000 signs and understands 2,000 words of spoken English.

For over 25 years, Koko has been helping scientists at the Gorilla Foundation. Workers there observe and record how gorillas think and act.

Koko's trainers hope to prove that gorillas are capable of thinking, feeling, and imagining things. They give Koko tests to determine how smart she is.

One year Koko was given a kitten. Koko cared for her pet, just as a human would.

When she was a college student, Penny Patterson taught Koko sign language.

Koko also likes to paint pictures. She has her own computer, and she chats on the Internet with her trainer's help. In these and other ways, she has shown that gorillas may be more like humans than we thought.

Some people disagree that Koko can think for herself and understand language like a human. They believe that she just copies what she sees.

The scientists at the Gorilla Foundation continue to communicate with Koko. They still are trying to find out if—and what—she really thinks and feels.

Koko using sign language today

Meet ELLEN LAMBETH

Ellen Lambeth writes for *Ranger Rick* magazine.

What do you like best about writing for Ranger Rick magazine?

Learning new stuff! Every time I work on an article, I first have to find out all I can about the topic. When working on "Do Animals Think?" I got to visit a zoo, watch animal behavior, talk to scientists, watch videos, and read, read, read. The more I learned, the more I wanted to know. It was hard work, but a lot of fun too!

Do you have any pets? If so, would you say that they "think"?

I have a dog—an Australian shepherd—and four Arabian horses. Although a lot of what they do is automatic, it's my opinion that they also can think. Of course, all of them can easily learn things I teach them. But every once in a while, I get a strong feeling that they are trying to teach ME something!

Do Animals THINK?

SOMETIMES THEY SEEM TO. IS THERE A WAY TO TELL FOR SURE?

By
Ellen
Lambeth

The Florida panther at right looks deep in thought. But don't let that pose fool you. Animals often do things that may make you *think* they're thinking.

Thinking about thinking is tricky, because thinking isn't something you can see. It goes on inside the brain. We know when *we're* doing it. But who can tell if an animal is thinking? It's not easy.

For example, check out these animal actions. Do they show that the animals are thinking—or not thinking? What do *you* think? (We'll tell you later what scientists think.)

- A bird builds a nest that's just right for its eggs and babies.
- An octopus uses its arms to open a jar with food inside.
- A lion sneaks around behind its prey and then chases it toward another lion that's hiding and waiting.
- A salmon returns from the ocean to the same stream where it hatched.

WHAT IS THINKING?

It may be easier to first explain what thinking *isn't*. For example, it isn't needed for things animals do automatically—like when a beaver dams a stream with sticks, mud, and grasses.

The beaver is making a pond, but it didn't learn how to do that. It doesn't think about doing it, either. Some animals just do what they do—kind of like robots—and they do it the same way every time. Scientists call this kind of behavior *instinct*.

But what about when an animal *does* learn something? Is that thinking? For example, you can teach a dog to give you its paw and "shake hands" for a treat.

Oops, excuse me. Sorry, pardon me. Don't mind me— just trying to get to the other side. Walking across the flock is just part of this sheepdog's job. Herding sheep gives the dog plenty to think about. It probably has its mind on what its next move will be to keep the sheep under control.

318

Even a worm can learn to follow a maze! But most scientists don't believe that the worm—or even the dog—is thinking when it learns such tricks.

A sheepdog at work, though, is a different story. One of the dog's jobs is to single out one sheep from a flock. The dog knows how to do that because it was trained.

But say the sheep doesn't want to leave the flock. It moves this way or that, or tries to duck behind another sheep. The dog must figure out a plan and keep changing that plan until it "outsmarts" the sheep, cutting it away from the others. Many people would agree that the sheepdog must be thinking about what it's doing.

THINKING TESTS

For a long time, scientists didn't study animal thinking. Most of them didn't believe that animals *could* think. They thought humans were the only thinking animals.

Now more scientists are studying this subject. But it's very hard to prove things that no one can see or measure. So some scientists decided to take a look at brains.

Is bigger better? No. Cow brains are bigger than dog brains, but that doesn't make cows smarter than dogs. And squirrels have some of the biggest brains of all for their body size. But squirrels aren't even close to being the smartest animals in the world. So the size of a brain may give some clues about brain power, but it doesn't prove anything.

Other scientists study thinking by watching how animals solve problems. They watch animals in the wild. Or they set up thinking tests in a lab.

For example, a scientist might put some food just out of an animal's reach. One kind of animal may grab a stick and use it to slide the food over. Another kind might not be able to figure out a way to get the food. Some scientists think animals that have lots of problems to solve must be smarter than animals with simple lives.

Scientists also study certain kinds of behavior for clues about thinking. They watch for three things: whether animals use tools, how they act with each other, and how they communicate. Here's a closer look....

TOOL TIME

People use lots of tools. We eat with forks and knives. We write with pens and pencils. We build with hammers and nails. There's just no end to the kinds of tools humans make and use.

But some other animals use tools too. The sea otter uses a stone to hammer open shellfish. An elephant uses a stick to scratch its back. And there's a kind of bird that uses a twig or cactus spine to poke out hidden insects.

Besides people, chimpanzees are the most famous tool-users. Like the bird, they use twigs to "fish" for insects. They also can make sponges out of leaves, use sticks and stones to crack open nuts, and wave branches around to scare off enemies.

Many scientists say tool use can be a sign of thinking—but not always. For instance, sea otters use their "hammers" out of instinct. They all do it—and they all do it the same way—even if they've never seen it done before.

The chimps are using plant stems to "fish" for termites. When some disturbed insects scurry up a stem, the chimp pulls it out to slurp up a crunchy treat. When animals use objects like this, it may mean that they are thinking.

But chimps seem to think about the tools they use. And they don't all use the same kinds of tools or use them in the same way.

For example, one chimp might notice some nuts and start looking around for a stick. It may check out several sticks and pick a certain one. Then it tries to crack a nut with it. If the stick doesn't do the trick, the chimp might change the stick somehow, pick out a different stick, or get a stone instead. Another chimp might discover that putting the nut on a rock first makes it easier to crack. This kind of problem solving is a good clue that thinking is going on.

GETTING ALONG

Some animals spend most of their lives alone. But others live in groups. An ant colony, for example, is made up of many, many ants. They all work together to find and store food, raise young, and keep the colony safe from enemies.

These ants seem to lead very complicated lives, but scientists would say that they're not thinking. Why? Because everything the ants do is just a pattern, an instinct. And they can't change that pattern, even if they need to.

Wolves live and work in groups too. They play together and howl together. They warn each other about trouble and help each other babysit. They also hunt together. Working as a team, they can track, chase, and kill prey much larger than themselves, such as moose.

Many scientists would say that, unlike the ants, wolves *do* think. That's because wolves can make plans and change their behavior, depending on what's going on around them.

ANIMAL TALK

Many animals communicate, or "talk"—with sounds, odors, colors, "body language," and other signals. Communication helps animals get along with each other and survive.

For example, honey bees do a dance in the hive that "tells" other bees where to find food. And birds sing songs that say, "This is *my* place!" Most scientists would say that this kind of "talking" is automatic and doesn't take any thinking.

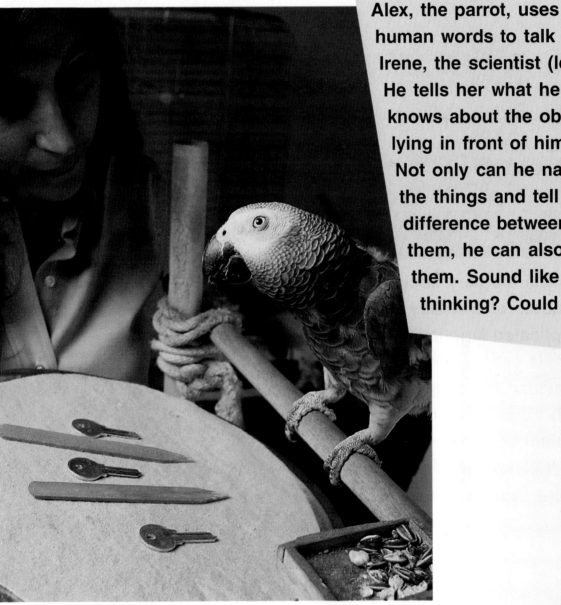

Alex, the parrot, uses human words to talk to Irene, the scientist (left). He tells her what he knows about the objects lying in front of him. Not only can he name the things and tell the difference between them, he can also count them. Sound like thinking? Could be.

Dolphins are very social. Scientists often study their complicated language. The animals seem to think through problems and cooperate with each other to solve them. These bottlenose dolphins (above) may be "talking over" some problem now—like what to do about the nosy photographer!

We *know* that human language takes thinking. So some scientists have tried to see what animals can do with our language. For example, a few apes have been taught sign language. The scientists who work with them say the apes seem to understand how the words work together. The apes sometimes even make up their own sentences. These could be clues that the animals are thinking.

And then there's Alex. Alex is an African gray parrot. Like any parrot, he can mimic the human voice. But this is one parrot that just might know what he's talking about!

Alex seems to understand and use human words in the correct way—not just copy them. That makes some people feel that Alex—and the apes that use sign language—must be thinking animals.

SO, THINK ABOUT IT

What did you decide about the animals in the beginning of this story? Well, the bird and salmon are using instinct. Their behaviors are amazing, but they stay the same, no matter what. The lion and octopus are most likely thinking. Why? Because each is carrying out some kind of crafty plan to solve a problem. And if things were different, they could change their plans and solve their problems in different ways.

More and more scientists are coming up with new ways to study animal brain power. They often disagree. But many are sure that we humans aren't the only thinkers. And that leaves us with plenty to think about!

Story Questions & Activities

1. What is one way that animals communicate?

2. Are animals with bigger brains always smarter?

3. Do you think animals can think? Explain.

4. What is the main idea of this selection?

5. Compare the ants in "Two Bad Ants" to the ants in this selection. How are they different? How are they the same?

Write a Tale

Write a tale about a group of animals who work together to solve a problem. Be sure your tale has a beginning, middle, and end.

Play Charades

Animals communicate with each other without using words. Play charades with a partner. Take turns trying to act out the title of a favorite book or movie. Hold up your fingers to show how many words are in the title.

Write an Animal Riddle

Choose an animal and look up facts about it. Then write an animal riddle on one side of a file card. A riddle about a wolf might say, *"I live in a pack. I eat meat. What kind of animal am I?"* Share your riddle with the class.

Find Out More

Find out more about an animal by doing some animal watching. You can observe a pet or go to a park with an adult to study animals that live there, such as birds.

Jot down what you notice about the animal's actions and the sounds it makes. Share your observations with the class.

Use an Encyclopedia Index

Most encyclopedias have a special volume for the **index**. You can use it to look up something and find out which volumes contain facts about that subject. For example, if you looked up birds, the information in the index might be something like this.

BIRCH — Guide Word

Topic

Birch B: 242

    Tree **T: 677** *with pictures*

    Wood **W: 845**

Bird B: 250 *with pictures*

    Animal **A: 179** — Volume

    Egg (Bird's Eggs) **E: 331** *with pictures*

    Molting **M: 483** — Page Number

    Pets **P: 281** *with pictures*

Use the index to answer these questions.

1 How is the information arranged in the index?

2 What volume would the topic *eggs* be found in?

3 Name a topic that appears under *birch*.

4 Which topics have pictures?

5 Where would you look for information about having a bird for a pet?

328

TEST POWER

Test Tip
Sometimes it helps to tell the story again in your own words.

DIRECTIONS:
Read the story. Then read each question about the story.

SAMPLE

Show-and-Tell Day

For Show-and-Tell Day, Jerry brought his pet turtle to school. No one in class had ever seen a live turtle!

"What does she like to eat?" Mary asked.

"She eats plants and lettuce," said Jerry. "Some other kinds of turtles eat small insects."

"What happens if she goes underwater?" Carlos asked.

Jerry picked up his turtle and put her back in her cage. "She can swim underwater and hold her breath for a long time," he explained. "If you watch her long enough, you'll see her stick her head above the water for air."

Just then, the turtle stuck her head out of the water. She breathed in air and then went back under the water again. Everyone in the class cheered!

1 In this story, Mary is —
   ○ jealous
   ○ quiet
   ○ curious
   ○ sad

2 Which of these is NOT a fact from the story?
   ○ The turtle eats lettuce.
   ○ Jerry's turtle eats insects.
   ○ The turtle holds her breath.
   ○ The turtle goes underwater.

Snap the Whip by Winslow Homer, 1872
Butler Institute of American Art, Youngstown, Ohio

Some paintings are filled with action. The people in the picture seem to move before our eyes. The painting seems to come to life.

Look at this painting. What can you tell about it? How do you think the boys feel? Do you think the artist enjoyed painting this picture? Give reasons why you think so.

Look at the painting again. What part of it do you find most interesting?

Draw Conclusions

Develop a strategy for drawing conclusions.

1. **Read the title.** What does it suggest the story will be about?

2. **Look at the events** in the story. What are the characters doing?

3. **Use your experience.** How would you feel if you were Duncan?

4. **Draw a conclusion.** Why do you think Duncan acted the way he did?

Swim, Duncan! Swim!

A small, ruffled, spluttering ball of yellow feathers plopped by the side of the stream.

"Why, hello, Duncan," said Carolina Cow. "What happened?"

"I was with my mother," Duncan sniffed, looking scared. "The wind carried me away, and now I'm lost."

"Your mom is just upstream. You can swim right to her."

"No, I can't," said Duncan. "Ever since I hurt my leg, mom has had to carry me everywhere."

"That was ages ago," Carolina said gently. "Your leg's healed now."

"If it's not, I'll drown!"

"Please try."

"No!" Duncan insisted. "I can't!"

"Okay," said Carolina. "Get up on my back and I'll carry you."

So Duncan climbed on and they entered the stream. Soon the water was up to the cow's back.

"Oh," said Carolina, "it's getting deeper and deeper and I can't swim."

"What should we do?" Duncan cried.

"You'd better swim for help."

Without thinking, Duncan jumped in and swam off. When he realized he was swimming, he turned back to thank Carolina. She was standing up. Duncan could see now that there had been no danger after all.

"You fooled me," he said, laughing.

"No," said Carolina. "You were only fooling yourself."

Meet E.B. White

E.B. White was born in 1899. He wrote his first children's book, *Stuart Little*, in 1945. The idea for *Charlotte's Web* began one day when White was on his farm. "I had been watching a big, gray spider at work and was impressed by how clever she was at weaving. Gradually I worked the spider into the story...a story of friendship."

In 1970, White won the Laura Ingalls Wilder Award for his contributions to children's literature. His three books for children, *Stuart Little*, *Charlotte's Web*, and *The Trumpet of the Swan*, are still read and loved today by children all over the world.

Meet Garth Williams

"Everybody in my home was always either painting or drawing," Garth Williams once said.

In 1945, Williams illustrated E.B. White's *Stuart Little,* which became an enormous success. This success made Williams decide to become a full-time illustrator of children's books. In the 1950s he illustrated *Charlotte's Web* and Laura Ingalls Wilder's *Little House on the Prairie* books. Among his most popular books were those written by George Selden, beginning with *The Cricket in Times Square*.

Wilbur's Boast

from
Charlotte's Web

by E.B. WHITE

Pictures by GARTH WILLIAMS

A spider's web is stronger than it looks. Although it is made of thin, delicate strands, the web is not easily broken. However, a web gets torn every day by the insects that kick around in it, and a spider must rebuild it when it gets full of holes. Charlotte liked to do her weaving during the late afternoon, and Fern liked to sit nearby and watch. One afternoon she heard a most interesting conversation and witnessed a strange event.

"You have awfully hairy legs, Charlotte," said Wilbur, as the spider busily worked at her task.

"My legs are hairy for a good reason," replied Charlotte. "Furthermore, each leg of mine has seven sections—the coxa, the trochanter, the femur, the patella, the tibia, the metatarsus, and the tarsus."

Wilbur sat bolt upright. "You're kidding," he said.

"No, I'm not, either."

"Say those names again, I didn't catch them the first time."

"Coxa, trochanter, femur, patella, tibia, metatarsus, and tarsus."

"Goodness!" said Wilbur, looking down at his own chubby legs. "I don't think *my* legs have seven sections."

"Well," said Charlotte, "you and I lead different lives. You don't have to spin a web. That takes real leg work."

"I could spin a web if I tried," said Wilbur, boasting. "I've just never tried."

"Let's see you do it," said Charlotte. Fern chuckled softly, and her eyes grew wide with love for the pig.

"O.K.," replied Wilbur. "You coach me and I'll spin one. It must be a lot of fun to spin a web. How do I start?"

"Take a deep breath!" said Charlotte, smiling. Wilbur breathed deeply. "Now climb to the highest place you can get to, like this." Charlotte raced up to the top of the doorway. Wilbur scrambled to the top of the manure pile.

"Very good!" said Charlotte. "Now make an attachment with your spinnerets, hurl yourself into space, and let out a dragline as you go down!"

Wilbur hesitated a moment, then jumped out into the air. He glanced hastily behind to see if a piece of rope was following him to check his fall, but nothing seemed to be happening in his rear, and the next thing he knew he landed with a thump. "Ooomp!" he grunted.

Charlotte laughed so hard her web began to sway.

"What did I do wrong?" asked the pig, when he recovered from his bump.

"Nothing," said Charlotte. "It was a nice try."

"I think I'll try again," said Wilbur, cheerfully. "I believe what I need is a little piece of string to hold me."

The pig walked out to his yard. "You there, Templeton?" he called. The rat poked his head out from under the trough.

"Got a little piece of string I could borrow?" asked Wilbur. "I need it to spin a web."

"Yes, indeed," replied Templeton, who saved string. "No trouble at all. Anything to oblige." He crept down into his hole, pushed the goose egg out of the way, and returned with an old piece of dirty white string. Wilbur examined it.

"That's just the thing," he said. "Tie one end to my tail, will you, Templeton?"

Wilbur crouched low, with his thin, curly tail toward the rat. Templeton seized the string, passed it around the end of the pig's tail, and tied two half hitches. Charlotte watched in delight. Like Fern, she was truly fond of Wilbur, whose smelly pen and stale food attracted the flies that she needed, and she was proud to see that he was not a quitter and was willing to try again to spin a web.

While the rat and the spider and the little girl watched, Wilbur climbed again to the top of the manure pile, full of energy and hope.

"Everybody watch!" he cried. And summoning all his strength, he threw himself into the air, headfirst. The string trailed behind him. But as he had neglected to fasten the other end to anything, it didn't really do any good, and Wilbur landed with a thud, crushed and hurt. Tears came to his eyes. Templeton grinned. Charlotte just sat quietly. After a bit she spoke.

"You can't spin a web, Wilbur, and I advise you to put the idea out of your mind. You lack two things needed for spinning a web."

"What are they?" asked Wilbur, sadly.

"You lack a set of spinnerets, and you lack know-how. But cheer up, you don't need a web. Zuckerman supplies you with three big meals a day. Why should you worry about trapping food?"

Wilbur sighed. "You're ever so much cleverer and brighter than I am, Charlotte. I guess I was just trying to show off. Serves me right."

Templeton untied his string and took it back to his home. Charlotte returned to her weaving.

"You needn't feel too badly, Wilbur," she said. "Not many creatures can spin webs. Even men aren't as good at it as spiders, although they *think* they're pretty good, and they'll *try* anything. Did you ever hear of the Queensborough Bridge?"

Wilbur shook his head. "Is it a web?"

"Sort of," replied Charlotte. "But do you know how long it took men to build it? Eight whole years. My goodness, I would have starved to death waiting that long. I can make a web in a single evening."

"What do people catch in the Queensborough Bridge—bugs?" asked Wilbur.

"No," said Charlotte. "They don't catch anything. They just keep trotting back and forth across the bridge thinking there is something better on the other side. If they'd hang head-down at the top of the thing and wait quietly, maybe something good would come along. But no—with men it's rush, rush, rush, every minute. I'm glad I'm a sedentary spider."

"What does sedentary mean?" asked Wilbur.

"Means I sit still a good part of the time and don't go wandering all over creation. I know a good thing when I see it, and my web is a good thing. I stay put and wait for what comes. Gives me a chance to think."

"Well, I'm sort of sedentary myself, I guess," said the pig. "I have to hang around here whether I want to or not. You know where I'd really like to be this evening?"

"Where?"

"In a forest looking for beechnuts and truffles and delectable roots, pushing leaves aside with my wonderful strong nose, searching and sniffing along the ground, smelling, smelling, smelling..."

"You smell just the way you are," remarked a lamb who had just walked in. "I can smell you from here. You're the smelliest creature in the place."

Wilbur hung his head. His eyes grew wet with tears. Charlotte noticed his embarrassment and she spoke sharply to the lamb.

"Let Wilbur alone!" she said. "He has a perfect right to smell, considering his surroundings. You're no bundle of sweet peas yourself. Furthermore, you are interrupting a very pleasant conversation. What were we talking about, Wilbur, when we were so rudely interrupted?"

"Oh, I don't remember," said Wilbur. "It doesn't make any difference. Let's not talk any more for a while, Charlotte. I'm getting sleepy. You go ahead and finish fixing your web and I'll just lie here and watch you. It's a lovely evening." Wilbur stretched out on his side.

Twilight settled over Zuckerman's barn, and a feeling of peace.

Story Questions & Activities

1. What does Wilbur boast that he can do?

2. How does Fern feel about Wilbur?

3. Why do you think that Charlotte and Wilbur are such good friends?

4. What is this story mainly about?

5. Look back at "Spiders at Work." What might Charlotte say to Diane Hoyt-Goldsmith,the author of that selection?

Write a Story

Write a funny story about an animal who tries to do something only another kind of animal can do. For example,you could tell a story about a horse who tries to fly like a bird. Be sure to describe the characters in your story clearly.

Make a Spider

Fold black construction paper in half. Lay your hand palm down along the folded edge. Trace your fingers (not your thumb!) with a white crayon. Cut out the outline, unfold it, and you have a spider! Roll the legs around a pencil to make them curvy like a spider's.

Make a Farm Diorama

Charlotte, Wilbur, and Templeton all live on a farm. Create a diorama of a farm scene. Use a shoebox and draw or cut out pictures of things you would see on a farm. You can include animals, insects, people, machines, or buildings.

Find Out More

Charlotte named the seven different sections of her leg. Find out the different parts of your leg. Are any parts the same as Charlotte's? Which ones? Draw a diagram of your leg and label the different parts.

343

Do an Electronic Subject Search

A card catalog contains **author**, **title**, and **subject cards**. Many libraries have computers that provide the same information. If you want to find out which books are available on a particular subject, you can do an electronic search.

1	Celsi, Teresa The Fourth Little Pig	Fic, Children's Room	© 1990
2	King-Smith, Dick Ace: The Very Important Pig	Fic, Children's Room	© 1990
3	King-Smith, Dick Babe, the Gallant Pig	Fic, Children's Room	© 1983
4	Peet, Bill Chester, the Worldly Pig	Fic, Children's Room	© 1965
5	Pitre, Felix Juan Bobo and the Pig A Puerto Rican Folktale	398.21, Children's Room	© 1993

Use the electronic search results to answer these questions.

1 Who is the author of the book *Chester, the Worldly Pig*?

2 In what year was *The Fourth Little Pig* published?

3 Where can all of the books from this search be found?

4 Which book by Dick King-Smith came out in 1990?

5 Would another subject search be the best way to find more books by Bill Peet? Explain.

Test Tip
A FACT is something that is true, is in the story, and is not an opinion.

DIRECTIONS:
Read the story. Then read each question about the story.

SAMPLE

Move for Grandmother

Marcy's grandmother visited one day and made an <u>announcement</u>. "I'm moving to Florida," she said. "It's time to move someplace warm."

"Are you sure you will like Florida?" Marcy asked.

"Not yet, dear," her grandmother replied. "But sometimes you've got to try something to see if you like it."

"Will you miss being here with us?" Marcy asked.

Her grandmother gave her a big hug and kiss. "Of course I will, sweetheart," she said. "But you can come visit anytime!"

1 Which of these is a FACT in this story?

○ Grandmother is moving to Florida.

○ Grandmother is very nice.

○ Marcy is moving to Florida.

○ Grandmother knows she will like Florida.

2 In this story, the word <u>announcement</u> is —

○ something that is said

○ what might happen

○ a loud fight

○ what someone thinks

Why are your answers correct?

Stories in Art

Koala by Ferdinand Bauer 1760–1826

This is a picture of two koalas. Koalas are found in Australia.

~

Look at this picture carefully. What can you tell about it? Do you think the artist wanted to make the koalas look real? Would this picture be helpful if someone had never seen a koala before? Why?

~

What else do you see in the picture besides the koalas? What do you like best about this picture?

Author's Purpose and Point of View

Develop a strategy for finding the author's purpose and point of view.

1 **Identify the author's purpose.** Is the purpose to inform? Has the author given facts and details about the subject?

2 **Look at the map.** Why do you think the author included it?

3 **Describe the point of view.** Can you tell if the author likes the subject? Why do you think so?

4 **Decide how you feel** about the subject. Do you agree with the author?

Nature's Strangest Mammal

Imagine an animal so strange that when a scientist named George Shaw first saw one in 1799, he didn't think it was real.

This creature was about the size of a cat. It walked on land like a lizard but swam in the water with webbed feet. It had a flat tail like a beaver and a bill like a duck. It laid eggs like a reptile, but fed its young with milk like a mammal. It had brown fur, not feathers. It had no teeth and no ears.

It had spurs coated with poison on its back feet.

How could scientists classify such an animal? Though scientists finally classified the platypus as a mammal, its unusual mix of features makes it a very special case.

The shy platypus lives only in eastern Australia. Laws protect the animal and its home from harm. People work to keep the rivers and creeks clean. If they succeed, then these wonderful and strange animals will have a safe home for many more years to come.

Coral Sea

Northern Territory

Derby

Queensland

South Australia

New South Wales

Sydney

Canberra

Victoria

Indian Ocean

Tasmania

TIME
FOR KIDS

The Koala Catchers

348

Climbing Trees to Save Furry Animals

High in the branches of a tree, a koala quietly eats a eucalyptus leaf. Suddenly, she hears flapping near her head. Is it a bird? A rope gently loops around her neck. It pulls snug against her fur.

Don't worry, the koala is not being harmed. She is being saved. On Kangaroo Island, Australia, there are too many koalas. The animals are running out of food. A group called Koala Rescue is moving the koalas so they will not go hungry.

Rescuers on Kangaroo Island use poles to get the koalas safely down from their tree homes.

A koala eats only eucalyptus leaves.

This koala is getting weighed. Scientists hope to keep track of the koalas over the next few years.

349

A HELPING HAND FOR KOALAS

During the 1920s, some people feared that Australia's koalas were disappearing. They wanted to help keep koalas safe. So 18 koalas were moved to Kangaroo Island. People thought the koalas might do better on the island, which had plenty of eucalyptus trees.

Since then, the number of koalas on Kangaroo Island has reached 5,000! That is good news. There is also bad news.

Koalas are picky eaters. They only eat eucalyptus leaves. Too many koalas in one spot strip the trees of leaves. The trees die. With no more leaves to eat, the koalas would starve.

CREATURES WITH SHARP CLAWS

To solve the problem, Koala Rescue first gets the koalas down from their tree homes. "It's not easy," says Drew Laslett of Koala Rescue. "They don't like being captured out of their trees."

Smile and say "Eucalyptus"! Five koalas line up to get their picture taken. They may be cute, but they are still wild animals with sharp claws.

AUSTRALIA

Relocation Area

Kangaroo Island

DAVE HIGGS/EPA; OPPOSITE PAGE: THE STOCK MARKET

Koalas are carefully placed in crates before they fly off to their new homes.

The rescuers must be very careful with the animals. "Koalas are wild animals!" says Laslett. They have big, sharp claws.

So far, Koala Rescue has moved about 650 of the furry animals to a new home filled with eucalyptus forests. Laslett says the koalas seem to do fine after the move. His group is also planting thousands of new trees for the animals to eat. "We're all about saving koalas and making sure the place they live in is safe." That's good news for the koalas and for the people who care about them.

FIND OUT MORE
Visit our website:
www.mhschool.com/reading

Based on an article in *TIME FOR KIDS*.

DID YOU KNOW?
VERY COOL KOALA FACTS

◆ Koalas spend almost all of their time in trees. They come down only to move to another tree.

◆ Koalas live only in Australia.

◆ Koalas have pouches. A baby stays in its mother's pouch for five or six months. Then it rides on its mother's back for another six months.

◆ Koalas sleep about 19 hours a day.

◆ When a koala is born, it is the size of a jellybean.

◆ Koalas communicate by making a noise that sounds like something between a snore and a burp.

Story Questions & Activities

1 Why were 18 koalas brought to Kangaroo Island during the 1920s?

2 Why are people taking koalas from Kangaroo Island now?

3 Why, do you think, did the author write an article about saving the koala bears? Explain.

4 What is the main idea of this selection?

5 If the farm from "Charlotte's Web" were located in Australia and a koala were to visit Wilbur, what might they talk about? Explain.

Write a Letter

Pretend that you are one of the koalas that lives on Kangaroo Island. You are being moved to a new place. Write a letter to another koala describing what it is like to be moved. Include interesting details.

Make an Animal Map

Koalas are native to Australia. What other animals are native to Australia? Draw a map of Australia and decorate it with pictures of animals that are found in different parts of the country. Label your drawings to identify each animal.

Create a Mobile

Australia is a continent. Draw the outline of each continent, cut them out, and label them. Write an interesting fact under the name of each continent. Make a mobile by attaching yarn to the top of each shape and then tying the other end of the yarn to a hanger.

Find Out More

What is a marsupial? Are they found only in Australia? How many kinds are there? Use an encyclopedia to find out more about marsupials. Report what you find out to the class.

STUDY SKILLS

Use a Resource

Different resources contain different types of information. The resource you select depends on the type of information you need to find. This chart shows some resources that are commonly used for research.

Newspaper
A newspaper contains current information about local, national, or international events.

Encyclopedia
A set of encyclopedias is a collection of volumes arranged alphabetically. Each is full of entries that give a lot of useful information on many subjects.

Dictionary
A dictionary is an alphabetical list of words with their definitions, pronunciations, histories, and other information.

Card Catalog
A card catalog is a file listing all the books, newspapers, magazines, and other materials a library owns.

Telephone
A telephone can be used to place calls to people who can answer your questions or to connect to the Internet to search for information.

Telephone Book
A telephone directory is an alphabetical listing of all the published telephone numbers in a certain area.

Use the chart to answer these questions.

1. Which resource would you use to find the meaning of *eucalyptus*?

2. Which resource would tell about current events occurring on Kangaroo Island?

3. Which resource would you use to write a report describing a typical day in the life of a koala?

4. A volunteer from Koala Rescue is speaking at your local library. What resources would you use to find out the exact date and time of the presentation? Explain.

5. What two resources could you use to find out about the different kinds of animals that live in Australia?

TEST POWER

Test Tip

Look for clues around the underlined word to help figure out what it means.

DIRECTIONS:

Read the story. Then read each question about the story.

SAMPLE

Michael's Decision

Michael has been given permission to get a pet. He is trying to decide if he wants a puppy or a kitten. He is looking at two posters in the park.

FREE TO GOOD HOME — KITTENS

Now is your chance to get a free kitten! They have fluffy long hair and blue eyes. They make great pets because they:
• are easy to take care of
• are very affectionate
• do not bark

FREE TODAY!
FRIENDLY PUPPIES NEED A NEW HOME

These are very cute puppies and one of them can be your best friend!

A puppy makes a good companion because it will play with you when you:
• ride your bike
• play frisbee
• go fishing

TAKE ONE HOME NOW!

1 What decision is Michael trying to make?

○ How to play frisbee

○ Which pet to bring home

○ Which story to read

○ Where to go to school

2 In the FRIENDLY PUPPIES ad, the word <u>companion</u> means —

○ someone who writes stories

○ a playmate

○ someone who rides a bike

○ a student

Why are your answers correct?

355

The Other Side of the Door

On the other side of the door
I can be a different me,
As smart and as brave and as funny or strong
As a person could want to be.
There's nothing too hard for me to do,
There's no place I can't explore
Because everything can happen
On the other side of the door.

On the other side of the door
I don't have to go alone.
If you come, too, we can sail tall ships
And fly where the wind has flown.
And wherever we go, it is almost sure
We'll find what we're looking for
Because everything can happen
On the other side of the door.

by Jeff Moss

Reading for

You get information from many sources such as television, newspapers, advertisements, and the Internet. In school, textbooks bring you information about different subjects. In this section, you will learn strategies to help you understand and use the many kinds of information that are a part of your everyday life.

Information

Contents

A five-step strategy that can help you to remember more of what you read is **SQRRR**. The letters SQRRR stand for Survey, Question, Read, Recite, and Review. This strategy can be helpful when you read science and social studies textbooks.

Survey ❭ **Question** ❭ **Read** ❭ **Recite** ❭ **Review**

Use SQRRR

① **Survey**, or look over, the article. Look at the pictures. Read titles, headings, and captions. Words in dark type show important information.

② **Ask yourself questions** as you read. For example, "How does this fact connect with what I have just read?"

③ **Then read and reread** to find details.

④ **Recite and review** by telling in your own words what you read, either aloud or in writing.

Ecosystems

Survey.
I'll scan this page, looking at the title and headings.

Question.
I'll keep this question in mind as I read.

Vocabulary

ecosystem
community

Read to Learn

Main Idea Ecosystems are made up of living and nonliving things.

What Makes Up an Ecosystem?

Plants and animals live with one another. They also depend on one another to stay alive. They depend on nonliving things, too, like rocks, soil, water, and air. Together, all the living and nonliving things in a place make up an **ecosystem** (EK·oh·sis·tuhm). Earth can be thought of as one large ecosystem. Earth also contains smaller ecosystems, such as grasslands, forests, deserts, oceans, and ponds.

All the living things in an ecosystem make up a **community** (kuh·MYEW·ni·tee).

Read and reread.
• The main idea will help me focus my reading.
• I'll add the definition of the vocabulary word *ecosystem* to my word list.

Recite/Review.
The answer to this question will help me summarize this lesson.

A population of zebras lives on the grassland.

Summarize What are some of the living and nonliving things in an ecosystem?

Roles for Plants and Animals

Vocabulary

oxygen

carbon dioxide

carbon dioxide and oxygen cycles

algae

Get Ready

What do these fish need to survive? What do these plants need to survive? Do you think they might need each other? What would you do to take care of the living things in an aquarium?

Process Skill

You make a model when you make something that represents objects or events.

Explore Activity

How Do Living Things Meet Their Needs?

Materials

gravel

guppy or goldfish

small water plants

2-L plastic drink bottle

bottom of another drink bottle with holes

fish food

Procedure

BE CAREFUL! Handle animals carefully.

1 **Make a Model** Put a 3-cm layer of gravel into the plastic drink bottle.

2 Fill the bottle half full of water. Anchor the plants into the gravel.

3 Cover the bottle with the bottom of another bottle. Do not place it in direct sunlight.

4 After two days gently place the fish into the bottle. Add a few flakes of fish food.

5 **Observe** Look at your ecosystem every day for two weeks. Feed the fish twice each week. Record your observations.

Drawing Conclusions

1 How has your ecosystem changed over the two weeks?

2 What did the fish need to survive? What did the plants need to survive?

Read to Learn

Main Idea Living things depend on one another in many ways.

How Do Living Things Use Air?

What do you need from the air around you? It is something that you can't see, but you take it in with every breath. It's a gas called **oxygen**. All living things need oxygen.

Animals get oxygen in different ways. Animals that live in water get their oxygen from the plants in the water. Plants need oxygen, too. They also need a gas called **carbon dioxide**.

Where do these gases come from? They come from plants and animals! Plants make oxygen, a gas that animals need. Animals give off carbon dioxide, a gas that plants need.

Trees give off oxygen.

Trees take in carbon dioxide.

Plants give off oxygen.

Fish take in oxygen.

Plants take in carbon dioxide.

Fish give off carbon dioxide.

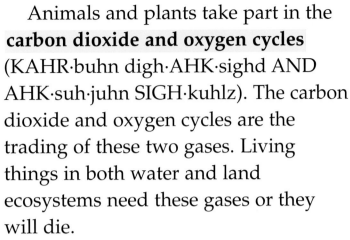

Animals and plants take part in the **carbon dioxide and oxygen cycles** (KAHR·buhn digh·AHK·sighd AND AHK·suh·juhn SIGH·kuhlz). The carbon dioxide and oxygen cycles are the trading of these two gases. Living things in both water and land ecosystems need these gases or they will die.

Where does the world's supply of oxygen come from? Plants in large forests make oxygen. Trees are the largest organisms that make oxygen. However, the most important source of oxygen lives in the oceans. Tiny one-celled organisms called **algae** make more oxygen than all the land plants in the world.

People take in oxygen.

People give off carbon dioxide.

Review Questions

1. How are you part of the carbon dioxide and oxygen cycles?

2. Compare the cycle of trading gases under water to the cycle of trading gases in the air.

3. What is the world's biggest supplier of oxygen?

Reading Research

When you write a report, you need to gather facts. You can look in books or magazines or on the Internet. One way to organize the facts you find is by taking notes. Notes give you a record of the information you gathered and of the sources where you found the information. Index cards are useful tools for collecting and organizing your facts.

Nonfiction Book

Take Notes

1 **Label your note cards.** At the top of each card, record your topic. Below that, write facts that relate to it.

2 **Identify your sources.** At the bottom of each card, write the author, editor (if any), title, city of publication, publisher, date, and page number. Include the address for Web sites, and any other details of your sources.

3 **Summarize your notes.** Rewrite the information from your cards in your own words. Be sure to use complete sentences.

4 **Organize your information.** Arrange your notes into categories based on the main ideas of your topic.

Washington, D.C., or the District of Columbia, lies on the east bank of the Potomac River. Across the river is Virginia. Maryland surrounds the capital city on the other three sides.

Topic: Washington, D.C.
D.C.= District of Columbia
East of Potomac River
Maryland on other 3 sides of D.C.

Jones, C.E. Our Nation's Capital. New York: McGraw-Hill, 2000. page 8.

Washington, D.C., is also called the District of Columbia. The city is east of the Potomac River. Virginia is on the other side of this river. Maryland borders the capital on three sides.

1 **Label your note cards.** I listed the topic and included some facts about it.

2 **Record the source.** This will remind me where my information came from.

3 **Summarize.** I will rewrite the notes I took in my own words and in complete sentences.

4 **Organize your information.** I will organize my notes based on the main ideas of my topic.

MY WILDEST RIDE

by Suzi Chong

Everyone knows Utah has some great slopes. That's why, when *Ski Fun* Magazine asked me to go there, I said yes right away! I've been skiing for 12 years, but I had never been to the Rocky Mountains.

Snow was falling during my drive from Salt Lake City to the slopes close to Park City. I could see why it had been chosen as the site of the 2002 Winter Olympics. It's beautiful! The minute I got there, I was ready to ski.

Topic: Skiing
Park City, Utah—good skiing
—ski resort near Salt Lake City
2002 Winter Olympics there

"My Wildest Ride"
by Suzi Chong
Ski Fun Magazine
August, 2002, pages 43—45

Park City, Utah, located not far from Salt Lake City, has some of the best skiing in the western United States. No wonder the area was chosen as the site of the 2002 Olympic Winter Games!

Brochure

Topic: Skiing
Western U.S.
Mogul Mountain
brochure 2002
Near Park City, Utah
rooms for 300 guests

New Snow Made Daily!

Come Ski with Us!

Located in Two Trees, Utah, near Park City and the 2002 Olympic Winter Games!

65 Trails for Beginners & Experts!

Mogul Mtn. Lodge, with rooms for 300, is located at the base of the ski area!

Great Dining and Shopping Nearby!

Review Questions

1. What complete sentence could you write using notes from the ski magazine article or the ad for Mogul Mountain?

2. What facts could you add to the notes taken for the Mogul Mountain brochure?

3. How does taking notes make it easier for you to write a report?

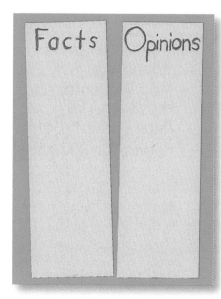

People get their information from many sources, which we call *media*. Newspapers, magazines, television, radio, and even flyers or posters are different kinds of media. Media give us information by presenting facts, which can be proved, or opinions, which are feelings or ideas. Using a chart can help you to keep track of facts and opinions as you read.

Look for Facts and Opinions

1. **Look for statements** that can be proved true. These are facts.

2. **Watch for clue words** such as *think*, *feel*, or *believe*. They tell you that a statement is an opinion.

3. **Use the facts and opinions** to learn about the issue or topic discussed.

4. **Form an opinion.** See which opinion the facts support best. Use the information presented to make up your own mind.

Poster

1 **Look for a statement** that is true. This statement is factual.

2 **Watch for clue words.** The word *believe* tells me this is an opinion.

3 **Use the facts and opinions.** I know these facts and opinions on the poster support one side of the issue.

4 **Form an opinion.** After listening to facts and opinions, I will make up my mind.

Town Meeting This Tuesday!

Help support the community garden

Join the Friends of Westwood Community Garden as we work to turn the Forest Street parking lot into a garden.

We believe Westwood has enough parking.
We need a garden!

A community garden will
* give 25 families their own garden plots.
* provide a beautiful space for all families.

Meet at Town Hall Tuesday 7:00 P.M. to learn more about it.

Newspaper Editorial

An editor, publisher, or owner of a newspaper writes an editorial. An editorial is usually about a current event or issue. Although editorials may contain facts, they are mainly the opinion or opinions of the newspaper staff.

Westwood Times
Editorial

Say Yes to Parking

This Tuesday, the Town Council will decide what to do with the rundown parking lot on Forest Street. Many business owners have asked the town to fix up the lot for public parking. However, the Friends of Westwood Community Garden want to plant a garden on the old lot. We at the *Westwood Times* think the town should support the businesses.

The number of businesses downtown is growing. Two parking lots have closed, and people often have to walk ten minutes to the stores after parking. Most people enjoy gardens, but we believe supporting our local businesses is more important. Please vote for the parking lot on Tuesday.

Television Debate

This week's Westwood Cable debate topic: Should the town repair the Forest Street parking lot or turn it into a community garden? Ellen Meara spoke for town businesses, and John Rivera spoke on behalf of the Friends of Westwood Community Garden.

Debate

Rivera: This is a perfect garden spot. Many people could use it.

Meara: If people can't park here, we believe businesses will close. The mall outside of town already takes away a lot of business from Westwood stores.

Rivera: The town has other parking choices. Why can't the town add another level to the parking lot on Main Street?

Meara: That plan would cost ten times more than fixing the old lot and lead to higher taxes.

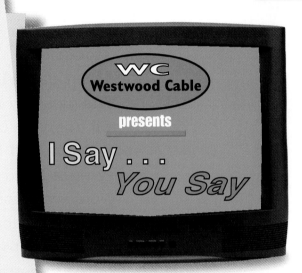

Review Questions

1. What facts are used by Ellen Meara in the TV debate. How do they support her argument?

2. Create a Fact and Opinion chart. Find the facts in the editorial and TV debate that are different from the ones in the poster. Add these to your chart. Do the same thing with any opinions you find.

3. Why is it important to be able to distinguish between facts and opinions in the media?

Glossary

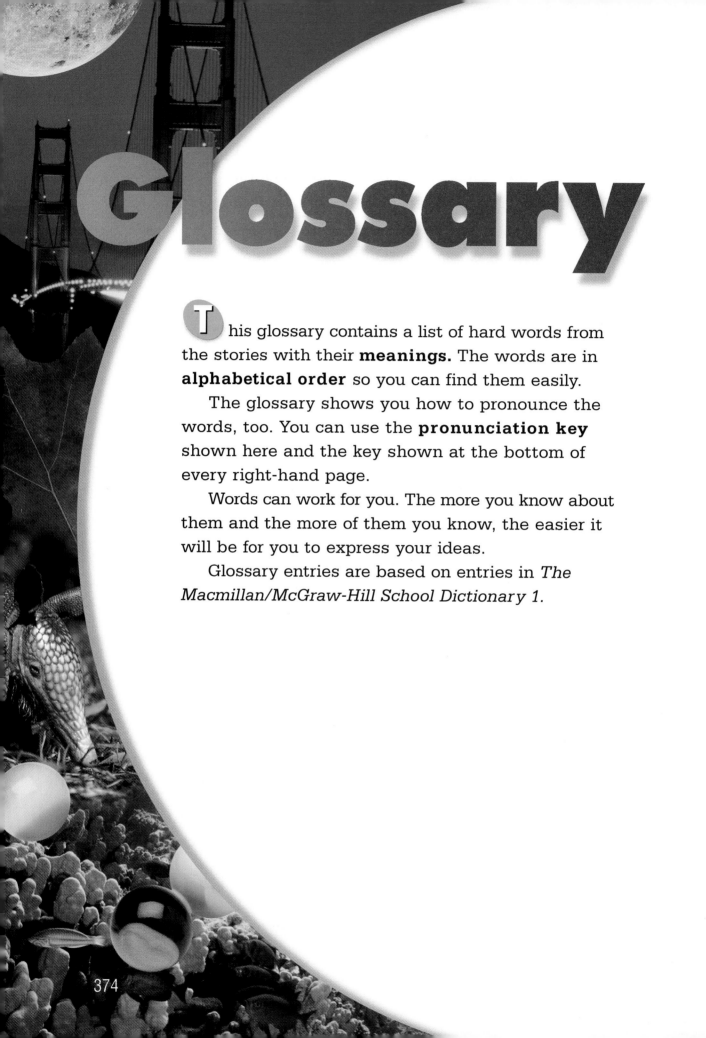

This glossary contains a list of hard words from the stories with their **meanings.** The words are in **alphabetical order** so you can find them easily.

The glossary shows you how to pronounce the words, too. You can use the **pronunciation key** shown here and the key shown at the bottom of every right-hand page.

Words can work for you. The more you know about them and the more of them you know, the easier it will be for you to express your ideas.

Glossary entries are based on entries in *The Macmillan/McGraw-Hill School Dictionary 1.*

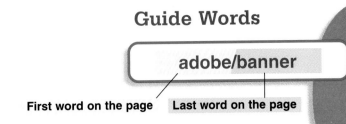
Sample Entry

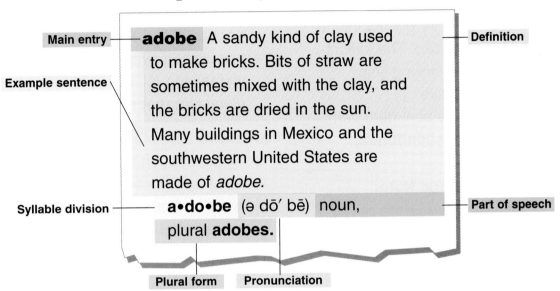

Main entry — **adobe** A sandy kind of clay used to make bricks. Bits of straw are sometimes mixed with the clay, and the bricks are dried in the sun. Many buildings in Mexico and the southwestern United States are made of *adobe*. — Definition

Example sentence

Syllable division — **a•do•be** (ə dō′ bē) noun, plural **adobes.** — Part of speech

Plural form | Pronunciation

a	at, bad	d	dear, soda, bad
ā	ape, pain, day, break	f	five, defend, leaf, off, cough, elephant.
ä	father, car, heart		
âr	care, pair, bear, their, where	g	game, ago, fog, egg
e	end, pet, said, heaven, friend	h	hat, ahead
ē	equal, me, feet, team, piece, key	hw	white, whether, which
i	it, big, English, hymn	j	joke, enjoy, gem, page, edge
ī	ice, fine, lie, my	k	kite, bakery, seek, tack, cat
îr	ear, deer, here, pierce	l	lid, sailor, feel, ball, allow
o	odd, hot, watch	m	man, family, dream
ō	old, oat, toe, low	n	not, final, pan, knife
ô	coffee, all, taught, law, fought	ng	long, singer, pink
ôr	order, fork, horse, story, pour	p	pail, repair, soap, happy
oi	oil, toy	r	ride, parent, wear, more, marry
ou	out, now	s	sit, aside, pets, cent, pass
u	up, mud, love, double	sh	shoe, washer, fish, mission, nation
ū	use, mule, cue, feud, few	t	tag, pretend, fat, button, dressed
ü	rule, true, food	th	thin, panther, both,
u̇	put, wood, should	t͟h	this, mother, smooth
ûr	burn, hurry, term, bird, word, courage	v	very, favor, wave
		w	wet, weather, reward
ə	about, taken, pencil, lemon, circus	y	yes, onion
b	bat, above, job	z	zoo, lazy, jazz, rose, dogs, houses
ch	chin, such, match	zh	vision, treasure, seizure

Aa

abandon To leave without intending to return; desert. The sailors *abandoned* the sinking ship.
▲ **Synonym**: leave
a•ban•don (ə ban′ dən) *verb*,
abandoned, abandoning.

> **Language Note:**.
> A **synonym** is a word that can be used instead of another word.
> A synonym for *abandon* is *desert*.

accept 1. To receive or admit, often with favor or approval. Our class *accepted* the new teacher immediately. **2.** To take something that is given. I *accepted* the birthday gift from my cousin.
ac•cept (ak sept′) *verb*,
accepted, accepting.

adult Having grown to full size; mature. An *adult* elephant is a huge animal.
a•dult (ə dult′ *or* ad′ ult) *adjective*.

advice An idea how to solve a problem or how to act in a certain situation. Our friends gave us *advice* about how to take care of a puppy.
ad•vice (ad vīs′) *noun*.

almanac A book that gives facts about the weather, the tides, and the rising and setting of the sun for every day of the year. *Almanacs* are published every year.
al•man•ac (ôl′ mə nak′) *noun*,
plural **almanacs**.

antenna One of a pair of long thin body parts, such as that on the head of an insect or a lobster. The beetle's *antennae* are on its head.
an•ten•na (an ten′ə) *noun*, *plural* **antennae**.

attack To begin to fight against with violence; assault. The enemy soldiers *attacked* the town at dawn. *Verb.* —The act of attacking. The *attack* on the fort came without warning. *Noun.*
at•tack (ə tak′) *verb*, **attacked, attacking**; *noun, plural* **attacks**.

avoid To keep away from. We took a back road to *avoid* the heavy highway traffic. ▲ **Synonyms**: escape, evade
a•void (ə void′) *verb,* **avoided, avoiding**.

Bb

baleen plates Tough, flexible bristles hanging from a whale's top jaw. Some whales have *baleen plates* instead of teeth.
> **ba•leen plates** (bə lēn′ plāts) *noun.*

batter To hit over and over again with heavy blows. The sailor was afraid the high waves would *batter* the small boat to pieces.
> **bat•ter** (bat′ ər) *verb,* **battered, battering.**

behavior A way of behaving or acting. The science students studied the *behavior* of grasshoppers.
> **be•hav•ior** (bi hāv′ yər) *noun,* *plural* **behaviors.**

belief A feeling that something is true, real, or worthwhile. My *belief* in my country is strong.
> **be•lief** (bi lēf′) *noun, plural* **beliefs.**

bitter Having a biting, harsh, bad taste. I did not like the *bitter* cough medicine.
> **bit•ter** (bit′ ər) *adjective.*

blubber A layer of fat under the skin of whales, seals, and some other sea animals. The oil made from whale *blubber* used to be burned in lamps.
> **blub•ber** (blub′ ər) *noun, plural.*

boast To talk too much or with too much pride about oneself; brag. Those two are always *boasting* of their good grades. *Verb.*
—A bragging statement. His *boast* that he can run fast is true. *Noun.*
> **boast** (bōst) *verb,* **boasted, boasting;** *noun, plural* **boasts.**

bob To move up and down or back and forth with a jerky motion. The ball *bobbed* on the waves.
> **bob** (bob) *verb,* **bobbed, bobbing.**

bore To make a hole in. The worm *bored* into the apple.
▲ Another word that sounds like this is **boar.**
> **bore** (bôr) *verb,* **bored, boring.**

at; āpe; fär; câre; end; mē; it; īce; pîerce; hot; ōld; sông; fôrk; oil; out; up; ūse; rüle; pùll; tûrn; chin; sing; shop; thin; this; hw in white; zh in treasure. The symbol ə stands for the unstressed vowel sound in about, taken, pencil, lemon, and circus.

bother To give trouble to; annoy. Noise *bothers* me when I study.
▲ **Synonyms:** pester, disturb
both•er (bo<u>th</u>′ ər) *verb,* **bothered, bothering.**

brain The large mass of nerve tissue inside the skull of persons and animals. The brain controls the actions of the body. The brain is also the center of thought, memory, learning, and the emotions.
brain (brān) *noun, plural* **brains.**

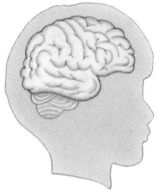

brief Short in time. My uncle is in town for a *brief* visit.
▲ **Synonym:** short
brief (brēf) *adjective.*

calm Not moving; still. The sea was *calm* after the storm.
▲ **Synonyms:** tranquil, peaceful
calm (käm) *adjective,* **calmer, calmest.**

clam An animal that has a soft body and a hinged shell in two parts. *Clams* are found in the ocean and in fresh water.
clam (klam) *noun, plural* **clams.**

claw A sharp, curved nail on the foot of a bird or animal. A cat has very sharp *claws.*
claw (klô) *noun, plural* **claws.**

cleat A projecting piece on the bottom of a shoe that gives it grip. I have *cleats* on my soccer shoes.
cleat (klēt) *noun, plural* **cleats.**

coal A black mineral that is burned as a fuel to heat buildings or make electricity. Coal is mostly carbon and is formed from decaying plants buried deep in the earth under great pressure.
coal (kōl) *noun, plural* **coals** *or* **coal.**

comfort To ease the sorrow or pain of someone. We tried to *comfort* the child by speaking to him softly.
▲ **Synonym:** console
com•fort (kum′ fərt) *verb,* **comforted, comforting.**

communicate To exchange or pass along feelings, thoughts, or information. I *communicated* with my friend by letter.
com•mu•ni•cate (kə mū′ ni kāt′) *verb,* **communicated, communicating.**

compare To study in order to find out how people or things are alike or different.
> **com•pare** (kəm pâr′) *verb,* **compared, comparing.**

completely Thoroughly, totally. The car was *completely* out of gas.
> ▲ **Synonym:** entirely
> **com•plete•ly** (kəm′ plēt′ lē) *adverb.*

conjunto A kind of band that plays drums, accordion, guitar and bass.
> **con•jun•to** (kən hün′ tō) *noun.*

consider To keep in mind. My grandparents are very healthy if you *consider* their age.
> **con•sid•er** (kən sid′ ər) *verb,* **considered, considering.**

conversation Talk between two or more persons. I had a long *conversation* with my friend.
> ▲ **Synonyms:** chat, discussion
> **con•ver•sa•tion** (kon′ vər sā′ shən) *noun, plural* **conversations.**

crafty Skillful in deceiving; sly; cunning. The *crafty* photographer took my picture when I didn't expect it.
> ▲ **Synonym:** sneaky
> **craft•y** (kraf′ tē) *adjective,* **craftier, craftiest.**

crate A box made of wooden slats. *Crates* are used to hold and protect things that are being stored.
> **crate** (krāt) *noun, plural* **crates.**

crystal Something that certain substances form when they change into a solid. Crystals have flat surfaces and a regular shape. Salt and snowflakes form into *crystals.*
> **crys•tal** (kris′ təl) *noun, plural* **crystals.**

curious Eager to know or learn. I was *curious* about snakes.
> ▲ **Synonym:** interested
> **cu•ri•ous** (kyur′ē əs) *adjective.*

Dd

delight To have or take great pleasure. My grandparents *delight* in telling us stories of their childhood.
> **de•light** (di līt′) *verb,* **delighted, delighting.**

design To make a plan, drawing, or outline of; make a pattern for. They *designed* costumes for the play. *Verb.*—An arrangement of shapes, parts, hair or colors; pattern. The quilt has a circular *design. Noun.*
> **de•sign** (di zīn′) *verb,* **designed, designing;** *noun, plural,* **designs.**

> at; āpe; fär; câre; end; mē; it; īce; pîerce; hot; ōld; sông; fôrk; oil; out; up; ūse; rüle; pùll; tûrn; chin; sing; shop; thin; **th**is; hw in white; zh in treasure. The symbol ə stands for the unstressed vowel sound in about, taken, pencil, lemon, and circus.

379

discover 1. To notice; come upon. I *discovered* a spelling error in my essay. 2. To see or find out for the first time. The explorer *discovered* a new pass through the mountains.
dis•cov•er (dis kuv′ ər) *verb*, **discovered, discovering.**

discuss To talk over, speak about. After dinner my friends and I *discussed* our plans for the future.
dis•cuss (di skus′) *verb*, **discussed, discussing.**

disguise To change the way one looks in order to hide one's real identity or to look like someone else. The children *disguised* themselves as pirates on Halloween. *Verb.*
—Something that changes or hides the way one looks. A mustache was part of the thief's *disguise. Noun.*
▲Synonym: costume
dis•guise (dis gīz′) *verb*, **disguised, disguising;** *noun, plural* **disguises.**

dozen A group of twelve. We bought three *dozen* donuts.
doz•en (duz′ən) *noun, plural* **dozens** *or* **dozen.**

drift Something that has been moved along or piled up by air or water currents. The storm caused *drifts* of snow 10 feet deep.
drift (drift) *noun, plural* **drifts.**

El Jardín (el har dēn′)

encourage To give courage, hope, or confidence to; urge on. The coach was *encouraging* the students to try out for the swimming team.
▲Synonym: urge
en•cour•age (en kûr′ ij,) *verb*, **encouraged, encouraging.**

energy The capacity for doing work. Some forms of energy are light, heat, and electricity. The windmill uses wind *energy.*
▲Synonym: power
en•er•gy (en′ ər jē) *noun, plural* **energies.**

entire Having all the parts; with nothing missing. Did you eat the *entire* cake?
▲Synonyms: whole, complete
en•tire (en tīr′) *adjective.*

equator An imaginary line around the Earth. It is halfway between the North and South Poles. The United States and Canada are north of the *equator.*
> **e•qua•tor** (i kwā′ tər) *noun, plural* **equators.**

equipment Anything that is provided for a particular purpose or use; supplies. The students bought some camping *equipment.*
> **e•quip•ment** (i kwip′ mənt) *noun.*

eucalyptus A tall evergreen tree or shrub that grows in warm climates. Wood from the *eucalyptus* is used to make floors and ships.
> **eu•ca•lyp•tus** (ū′ kə lip′ təs) *noun, plural* **eucalyptus.**

expect To think, suppose. We *expected* they would be late because of the traffic.
> **ex•pect** (ek spekt′) *verb,* **expected, expecting.**

experiment A test that is used to discover or prove something by watching results very carefully. The class did an *experiment* to show that fire needs oxygen to burn. *Noun.* —To make an experiment or experiments. Scientists tested the new drug by *experimenting. Verb.*
> **ex•per•i•ment** (ek sper′ ə mənt) *noun, plural* **experiments;** *verb,* **experimented, experimenting.**

expert A person who knows a great deal about some special thing. Veterinarians are animal *experts.*
> ▲**Synonyms:** pro, master
> **ex•pert** (ek′ spûrt) *noun, plural* **experts.**

fable 1. A made-up or untrue story. Have you heard the old *fable* that porcupines can shoot their quills? 2. A story that is meant to teach a lesson. Characters in *fables* are often animals that act like people.
> **fa•ble** (fā′ bəl) *noun, plural* **fables.**

---

at; āpe; fär; câre; end; mē; it; īce; pîerce; hot; ōld; sông; fôrk; oil; out; up; ūse; rüle; pu̇ll; tûrn; chin; sing; shop; thin; this; hw in white; zh in treasure. The symbol ə stands for the unstressed vowel sound in about, taken, pencil, lemon, and circus.

feast To have a feast; eat richly. We *feasted* on turkey and stuffing on Thanksgiving. *Verb.*
—A large, rich meal on a special occasion. After the wedding, the two families gathered for a *feast. Noun.*
feast (fēst) *verb,* **feasted, feasting;** *noun, plural* **feasts.**

frequently Happening often; taking place again and again. *Frequently,* there are thunderstorms here in the summer.
fre•quent•ly (frē′ kwənt lē) *adverb.*

funnel A utensil that has a wide cone at one end and a thin tube at the other. You can use a *funnel* to pour something into a container with a small opening without spilling.
fun•nel (fun′ əl) *noun, plural* **funnels.**

Word History:.

The word **funnel** comes from a Latin word meaning *to pour into.*

furious Very angry. My folks were *furious* when we missed the train by one minute.
▲**Synonyms:** mad, angry
fu•ri•ous (fyùr′ ē əs) *adjective.*

future The time that is to come. In the *future,* we may be able to visit the moon.
fu•ture (fū′ chər) *noun.*

gain To get or develop as an increase or addition. We need to *gain* three more points in the last inning to win the game.
gain (gān) *verb,* **gained, gaining.**

gingko A tree with fan-shaped leaves and yellow fruit. The *gingko* is native to Eastern China.
ging•ko (ging′ kō) *noun, plural* **gingkoes.**

gradual Happening little by little; moving or changing slowly. We watched the *gradual* growth of the seeds into plants in our vegetable garden.
grad•u•al (graj′ü əl) *adjective.*

grip To take hold of firmly and tightly. I *gripped* the suitcase and carried it off the train.
▲**Synonyms:** grasp, clutch
grip (grip) *verb,* **gripped, gripping.**

Hh

haughtily Thinking of oneself as much better than other people; in an arrogant way. Michael *haughtily* said "no" when he was asked to join the younger boys' game.
haught•i•ly (hô′ tə lē) *adverb.*

hero A person who is looked up to by others because of his or her great achievements or fine qualities. The swimmer who saved the child from drowning was a *hero*.
he•ro (hîr′ ō) *noun, plural* **heroes.**

hesitate To wait or stop a moment, especially because of feeling unsure. The speaker *hesitated* and looked at his notes.
▲Synonym: pause
hes•i•tate (hez′ i tāt′) *verb,* **hesitated, hesitating.**

human 1. A person. The boy had been raised by wolves and had never even seen another *human*. *Noun.* 2. Being or having to do with a person or persons. Men, women, and children are *human* beings. *Adjective.*
hu•man (ū′ mən) *noun, plural* **humans;** *adjective.*

hurl To throw hard and fast; fling. The pitcher turned and *hurled* the ball to first base.
hurl (hûrl) *verb,* **hurled, hurling.**

hurricane A storm with very strong winds and heavy rain. The weather forecast said a *hurricane* was forming to the north of Puerto Rico.
hur•ri•cane (hûr′ i kān′ *or* hur′ i kān′) *noun, plural* **hurricanes.**

inning One of the parts into which a baseball or softball game is divided. The team won the game in the ninth *inning*.
in•ning (in′ ing) *noun, plural* **innings.**

at; āpe; fär; cåre; end; mē; it; īce; pîerce; hot; ōld; sông; fôrk; oil; out; up; ūse; rüle; púll; tûrn; chin; sing; shop; thin; this; hw in white; zh in treasure. The symbol ə stands for the unstressed vowel sound in about, taken, pencil, lemon, and circus.

insect Any of a large group of small animals without a backbone. The body of an insect is divided into three parts. Insects have three pairs of legs and usually two pairs of wings. Flies, ants, grasshoppers, and beetles are *insects*.
    in•sect (in′ sekt) *noun, plural* **insects.**

Word History:

The word **insect** comes from a Latin word that means "cut into." An insect was called "an animal that has been cut into" because its body is divided into three sections.

---

instinct A way of acting or behaving that a person or animal is born with and does not have to learn. Birds build nests by *instinct*.
    in•stinct (in′ stingkt) *noun, plural* **instincts.**

insulate To cover or surround with a material that slows or stops the flow of electricity, heat, or sound. The electrician *insulated* the electric wires with rubber. Our house is *insulated* so that it stays warm inside in the winter.
    ▲**Synonyms:** shield, protect
    in•su•late (in′ sə lāt′) *verb,* **insulated, insulating.**

integrate 1. To make open to people of all races. The town *integrated* all its schools long ago. **2.** To bring parts together into a whole. The reporter tried to *integrate* all the different accounts of the accident into one clear story.
    in•te•grate (in′ ti grāt′) *verb,* **integrated, integrating.**

interrupt To break in upon or stop a person who is acting or speaking. Please do not *interrupt* me when I'm talking.
    in•ter•rupt (in′ tə rupt′) *verb,* **interrupted, interrupting.**

invisible Not able to be seen; not visible. Oxygen is an *invisible* gas.
    in•vis•i•ble (in vis′ ə bəl) *adjective.*

kingdom A country that is ruled by a king or a queen.
    king•dom (king′ dəm) *noun, plural* **kingdoms.**

koala A furry, chubby animal that lives in Australia. *Koalas* are marsupials.
    ko•a•la (kō ä′ lə) *noun, plural* **koalas.**

krill Tiny, pale pink, shrimp-like creatures the size of a person's little fingers. Whales eat *krill*.
krill (kril) *noun.*

label A piece of cloth, paper, or other material that is fastened to something and gives information about it. The *label* inside the shirt tells the brand name. *Noun* —To put a label on. I can label the package you want to mail. *Verb*
la•bel (lā′ bəl) *noun, plural* **labels;** *verb,* **labeled, labeling.**

loop To make a rounded shape formed by the part of a string, wire, or rope that crosses itself. She *loops* the laces of her sneakers.
loop (lüp) *verb* **looped, looping.**

Lon Po Po (lon pô pô)

magnify 1. To make something look bigger than it really is. The microscope *magnified* the cells.
▲**Synonyms:** enlarge, increase
mag•ni•fy (mag′ nə fī′) *verb,* **magnified, magnifying.**

mammal A kind of animal that is warm-blooded and has a backbone. Human beings, cattle, dogs, cats, and whales are *mammals*.
mam•mal (mam′ əl) *noun, plural* **mammals.**

meal¹ The food served or eaten at one time. Breakfast is the first *meal* of the day.

meal² Grain or other food that has been ground. I mixed corn *meal* into the batter.
meal (mēl) *noun, plural* **meals.**

member A person, animal or thing that belongs to a group. The club has ten *members*.
mem•ber (mem′ bər) *noun, plural* **members.**

at; āpe; fär; câre; end; mē; it; īce; pîerce; hot; ōld; sông; fôrk; oil; out; up; ūse; rüle; pùll; tûrn; chin; sing; shop; thin; this; hw in white; zh in treasure. The symbol ə stands for the unstressed vowel sound in about, taken, pencil, lemon, and circus.

mesquite A tree or shrub native to the Southwestern United States and Mexico. Wood from the *mesquite* tree is fragrant.
   mes•quite (mes kēt′) *noun.*

mimic To imitate, especially in order to make fun of. The comedian could *mimic* people's voices.
   mim•ic (mim′ ik) *verb,* **mimicked, mimicking;** *noun, plural* **mimics.**

mistake Something that is not correctly done, said, or thought. I made two *mistakes* on the test.
   ▲ **Synonym:** error
   mis•take (mis tāk′) *noun, plural* **mistakes.**

model A small-sized copy of something. I made this airplane *model* from a kit. *Noun.*
   —To make or design something. The sculptor uses a tool to *model* clay. *Verb.*
   mod•el (mod′ əl) *noun, plural* **models;** *verb,* **modeled, modeling.**

motion The act of changing place or position; movement. The batter made a swinging *motion.*
   ▲ **Synonym:** action
   mo•tion (mō′ shən) *noun.*

nectar The sweet liquid formed in flowers. Bees use *nectar* to make honey.
   nec•tar (nek′ tər) *noun, plural* **nectars.**

nopalitos Edible, freshly cut cactus pads. We made a salad using *nopalitos.*
   no•pa•li•tos (nō pə lē′ tōz) *noun, plural.*

ostrich A large bird that has a long neck, long, strong legs, and a small flat head. The ostrich is the largest of all living birds. It cannot fly, but it can run very fast.
   os•trich (ôs′ trich *or* os′ trich) *noun, plural* **ostriches.**

Pp

pace 1. To walk back and forth across. The tiger *paced* its cage.
   pace (pās) *verb,* **paced, pacing.**

paloverde A tree native to the desert. *The cactus was protected from the sun and wind by the paloverde tree.*
pal•o•ver•de (pal ō vâr′ dā) *noun.*

Paotze (pou′ dze)

pennant A long, narrow flag that is shaped like a triangle. *Pennants are used for signaling and as emblems, decorations, and prizes.*
pen•nant (pen′ ənt) *noun, plural* **pennants.**

perform To sing, act, or do something in public that requires skill. *Our band performed at the game.*
per•form (pər fôrm′) *verb,* **performed, performing.**

period¹ A portion of time. *They were on vacation for a period of six weeks.*

period² A punctuation mark (.) used at the end of a declarative or an imperative sentence, or at the end of an abbreviation. *This sentence needs a period at the end of it.*
pe•ri•od (pîr′ ē əd) *noun, plural* **periods.**

persist To continue firmly and steadily. *The rainy weather persisted all week.*
▲ **Synonyms:** continue, last
per•sist (pər sist′) *verb,* **persisted, persisting.**

piñata a colorfully decorated container originally used in Latin-American Christmas and birthday celebrations. It is filled with fruit, candy, and gifts and hung by a string. *The boy hit the piñata and broke it open.*
pi•ña•ta (pēn yä′ tə) *noun, plural,* **piñatas.**

pollution 1. The act or process of polluting. *Pollution is a major problem in many of our cities.* 2. Harmful materials such as certain gases, chemicals, and wastes.
pol•lu•tion (pə lü′ shən) *noun.*

at; āpe; fär; câre; end; mē; it; īce; pîerce; hot; ōld; sông; fôrk; oil; out; up; ūse; rüle; pu̇ll; tûrn; chin; sing; shop; thin; this; hw in white; zh in treasure. The symbol ə stands for the unstressed vowel sound in about, taken, pencil, lemon, and circus.

387

porcupine A forest animal whose body is covered with sharp quills.
por•cu•pine (pôr′ kyə pīn′) *noun, plural* **porcupines.**

Word History:

The word **porcupine** comes from the Latin word for *pig* and the Latin word *spines*. A *porcupine* is round and chubby like a pig, and its quills are like sharp spines.

portion An amount of food served to one person. Each of us had a *portion* of the potatoes.
por•tion (pôr′ shən) *noun, plural* **portions.**

powdered Made into fine bits by grinding, crushing, or crumbling. Sometimes you can use *powdered* milk for recipes.
pow•dered (pou′ dərd) *adjective.*

printer 1. A person or company whose business is to *print* books, magazines, or other material. 2. An instrument that can be connected to a computer to produce a *printed* copy of a file that is stored on a disk.
prin•ter (prin′ tər) *noun, plural,* **printers.**

produce To make or create something. Cows *produce* milk.
▲ **Synonym:** make
pro•duce (prə düs′ *or* prə dūs′) *verb,* **produced, producing.**

Queensborough Bridge
(kwēnz′ bûr ō brij′)

rapidly Very quickly; fast. The train traveled *rapidly* down the track.
▲ **Synonyms:** swiftly, speedily
ra•pid•ly (rap′ id lē) *adverb.*

relative A person who belongs to the same family as someone else. Tim and his cousin are *relatives.*
re•la•tive (rel′ ə tiv) *noun, plural* **relatives.**

remain 1. To be left. All that *remains* of the ancient city is ruins. 2. To stay behind in the same place. I *remained* at home.
re•main (ri mān′) *verb,* **remained, remaining.**

reply Something said, written, or done in answer. You gave the correct *reply* to the teacher's question. *Noun.*
—To answer in speech, writing or action. The mayor *replied* to my letter. *Verb.*
> **re•ply** (ri plī′) *noun, plural* **replies;** *verb,* **replied, replying.**

report An account, statement, or announcement, often formal or prepared for the public. I wrote a book *report. noun.*
> **re•port** (ri pôrt′) *noun, plural* **reports.**

rescuer Someone who saves or frees people or animals. The cat *rescuers* took in some strays from the street.
> **res•cu•er** (res′ kū ər) *noun, plural* **rescuers.**

rib 1. Something that looks like or acts as a *rib.* An umbrella has *ribs.* **2.** One of the curved bones that are attached to the backbone and curve around to enclose the chest cavity. The *ribs* protect the heart.
> **rib** (rib) *noun, plural* **ribs.**

route A road or other course used for traveling. We drove along the ocean *route* to the beach.
> ▲ Another word that sounds like this is **root.**
> **route** (rüt *or* rout) *noun, plural* **routes.**

saguaro A tall, sparsely branched cactus native to the Southwestern United States and Mexico. The *saguaro* has spiny branches.
> **sa•guar•o** (sə gwär′ō *or* sə wär′ō) *noun, plural* **saguraros.**

sanitation The protection of people's health by keeping living conditions clean. *Sanitation* includes getting rid of garbage.
> **san•i•ta•tion** (san′ i tā′ shən) *noun.*

scientific Having to do with or used in science. The students had to plan a *scientific* experiment.
> **sci•en•tif•ic** (sī′ ən tif′ ik) *adjective.*

at; āpe; fär; câre; end; mē; it; īce; pîerce; hot; ōld; sông; fôrk; oil; out; up; ūse; rüle; pu̇ll; tûrn; chin; sing; shop; thin; this; hw in white; zh in treasure. The symbol ə stands for the unstressed vowel sound in about, taken, pencil, lemon, and circus.

screech To make a shrill, harsh cry or sound. The monkeys *screeched* at feeding time. The car's brakes *screeched*.
▲ **Synonyms:** shriek, squawk, scream
screech (skrēch) *verb,* **screeched.**

sedentary Doing or requiring much sitting. Not active. After surgery, the patient was told to remain *sedentary* for two weeks.
se•den•tary (sed′ ən ter′ē) *adjective.*

seize **1.** To take hold of; grab. The dog *seized* the bone. **2.** To get control of; capture. The soldiers *seized* the fort.
▲ Two words that sound like this are **sees** and **seas**.
seize (sēz) *verb,* **seized, seizing.**

Shang (shang *or* shong)

snug Fitting very closely or tightly. Even though this sweater is a bit *snug*, I can still wear it.
▲ **Synonym:** tight
snug (snug) *adjective.*

social Living together in organized communities. A bee is a *social* insect.
so•cial (sō′ shəl) *adjective.*

solar **1.** Using or powered by the energy of the sun. This *solar* car uses sunshine for energy. **2.** Having to do with or coming from the sun. *Solar* energy is sometimes used for heating homes.
so•lar (sō′ lər) *adjective.*

solve To find the answer to. I *solved* all the arithmetic problems correctly.
solve (solv) *verb,* **solved, solving.**

spinneret An organ for producing silk threads through the secretion of silk glands. Spiders and caterpillars have *spinnerets*.
spin•ner•et (spin′ ə ret′) *noun,* *plural* **spinnerets.**

starve To suffer from or die of hunger. Some people feed the birds in winter so they don't *starve*.
starve (stärv) *verb,* **starved, starving.**

strip To pull off. We need to *strip* the bark from this log.
strip (strip) *verb,* **stripped, stripping.**

stun To make unconscious. The robin was *stunned* when it flew into the window.
▲ **Synonym:** knock out
stun (stun) *verb,* **stunned, stunning.**

subject 1. Something thought or talked about. The *subject* of the student's report was birds' nests. **2.** A course or field that is studied. Math is my favorite *subject* in school.
> **sub•ject** (sub′jikt) *noun, plural* **subjects.**

swallow¹ To cause food to pass from the mouth to the stomach. The tiger chewed the meat and then *swallowed* it.
> **swal•low** (swol′ ō) *verb,* **swallowed, swallowing.**

swallow² A small bird with long wings. *Swallows* are very good fliers.
> **swal•low** (swol′ ō) *noun, plural* **swallows.**

switch To change. We *switched* seats on the bus ride home.
> ▲ **Synonyms:** swap, trade
> **switch** (swich) *verb,* **switched, switching.**

talented Having or showing *talent.* She is a very *talented* dancer.
> ▲ **Synonyms:** gifted, skillful
> **tal•ent•ed** (tal′ ən tid) *adjective.*

Tao (tou *or* dou)

temperature The degree of heat or cold. *Temperature* is often measured with a thermometer. The *temperature* outside is going down.
> **tem•per•a•ture** (tem′ pər ə chər) *noun, plural* **temperatures.**

tough 1. Not easy to break, cut, or damage; strong. Canvas is a *tough* cloth. **2.** Able to put up with difficulty, strain, or hardship. The pioneers had to be *tough.*
> **tough** (tuf) *adjective,* **tougher, toughest.**

translate To say in or change into another language. The class had to *translate* the story from English to French.
> **trans•late** (trans lāt′) *verb,* **translated, translating.**

> at; āpe; fär; câre; end; mē; it; īce; pîerce; hot; ōld; sông; fôrk; oil; out; up; ūse; rüle; pu̇ll; tûrn; chin; sing; shop; thin; <u>th</u>is; hw in white; zh in treasure. The symbol ə stands for the unstressed vowel sound in about, taken, pencil, lemon, and circus.

391

treat Something that is a special pleasure. Going to the circus was a *treat*.

    treat (trēt) *noun, plural,* **treats.**

triumphant Successful or victorious. Our team was *triumphant* in the game.

    tri•um•phant (trī um′ fənt) *adjective.*

Uu

unbearably In a way that is unendurable or unable to be tolerated. The noise near the runway was *unbearably* loud.

    un•bear•a•bly (un bâr′ ə blē) *adverb.*

Vv

vanish To go out of sight or existence. The airplane *vanished* above the clouds.

  ▲ **Synonym:** disappear
    van•ish (van′ ish) *verb,* **vanished, vanishing.**

vast Very great in size or amount. That ranch covers a *vast* area.

  ▲ **Synonym:** immense
    vast (vast) *adjective.*

Ww

weight The amount of heaviness of a person or thing. My *weight* is 70 pounds.

  ▲ Another word that sounds like this is **wait.**
    weight (wāt) *noun, plural* **weights.**

whirling Turning around quickly in a circle. The *whirling* leaves fell down around me.

  ▲ **Synonym:** spinning
    whirl•ing (hwûrl′ ing *or* wûrl′ ing) *adjective.*

wit The ability to make clever, amusing, and unusual comments. The speaker's *wit* delighted and stimulated the audience.

    wit (wit) *noun.*

ACKNOWLEDGMENTS

The publisher gratefully acknowledges permission to reprint the following copyrighted material:

"Animal Fact/Animal Fable" from ANIMAL FACT/ANIMAL FABLE by Seymour Simon, illustrated by Diane de Groat. Text copyright © 1979 by Seymour Simon. Illustrations copyright © 1979 by Diane de Groat. Reprinted by permission of Crown Children's Books, a division of Random House, Inc.

"The Bat Boy and His Violin" by Gavin Curtis. Text copyright © 1998 by Gavin Curtis. Illustrations copyright © 1998 by Earl B. Lewis. Reprinted by permission of Simon & Schuster Books for Young Readers. Simon and Schuster Children's Publishing Divisions. All rights reserved.

Cover permission for BICYCLE RIDER by Mary Scioscia; illustrated by Ed Young. Illustrations copyright © 1983 by Ed Young. Reprinted by permission of HarperCollins Publishers.

"Big Blue Whale" by Nicola Davies. Text copyright © 1997 by Nicola Davies. Illustrations copyright © 1997 by Nick Maland. Reprinted by permission of Candlewick Press, Inc., Cambridge, MA.

"Cactus Hotel" from CACTUS HOTEL text by Brenda Z. Guiberson, illustrated by Megan Lloyd. Text copyright © 1991 by Brenda Guiberson. Illustrations copyright © 1991 by Megan Lloyd. Reprinted by permission of Henry Holt and Co.

"Wilbur's Boast" from CHARLOTTE'S WEB by E. B. White. Copyright © 1952 by E. B. White. Text copyright renewed 1980 by E. B. White. Illustrations copyright renewed 1980 by Garth Williams. Reprinted by permission of HarperTrophy, a division of HarperCollins Publishers

"Cloudy With a Chance of Meatballs" is from CLOUDY WITH A CHANCE OF MEATBALLS by Judi Barrett. Text copyright © 1978 by Judi Barrett. Illustrations copyright © 1978 by Ron Barrett. Reprinted with permission of Atheneum Books for Young Readers, Simon & Schuster Children's Publishing Division.

"Do Animals Think?" by Ellen Lambeth reprinted from the March 1997 issue of RANGER RICK magazine, with the permission of the publisher, the National Wildlife Federation. Copyright © 1997 by the National Wildlife Federation.

"Do Oysters Sneeze?" by Jack Prelutsky from THE NEW KID ON THE BLOCK by Jack Prelutsky. Text copyright © 1984 by Jack Prelutsky. Used by permission of HarperCollins Publishers.

"Dreams" by Langston Hughes from COLLECTED POEMS by Langston Hughes. Copyright © 1994 by the Estate of Langston Hughes. Reprinted by permission of Alfred A. Knopf, Inc.

"A Fly and a Flea in a Flue" by P. L. Mannock from THE KINGFISHER BOOK OF CHILDREN'S POETRY. Text copyright © 1993. Reprinted by permission of Kingfisher Books.

Cover permission for THE GIRL WHO LOVED THE WIND by Jane Yolen; illustrated by Ed Young. Illustrations copyright © 1972 by Ed Young. Reprinted by permission of HarperCollins Publishers.

"I Can" by Mari Evans from SINGING BLACK by Mari Evans. Text copyright © 1976 by Mari Evans, published by Reed Visuals, © 1979. Reprinted by permission of the author.

"In My Family" by Carmen Lomas Garza. Copyright © 1996 by Carmen Lomas Garza. Reprinted with permission of the publisher, Children's Book Press, San Francisco, CA.

"Lon Po Po: A Red-Riding Hood Story from China" is from LON PO PO: A RED-RIDING HOOD STORY FROM CHINA translated and illustrated by Ed Young. Copyright © 1989 by Ed Young. Reprinted by permission of Philomel Books.

"The Many Lives of Benjamin Franklin" by Aliki. Copyright © 1988 by Aliki Brandenburg. Reprinted by permission of Simon & Schuster Books for Young Readers, Simon & Schuster Children's Publishing Division. All rights reserved.

"The Other Side of the Door" from THE OTHER SIDE OF THE DOOR by Jeff Moss. Copyright © 1991 by Jeff Moss. Used by permission of Bantam Books, a division of Random House, Inc.

"The Terrible EEK" from THE TERRIBLE EEK. Text copyright © 1991 by Patricia A. Compton. Illustration copyright © 1991 by Sheila Hamanaka. Reprinted with permission of Simon & Schuster Books for Young Readers, Simon & Schuster Children's Publishing Division. All rights reserved.

"Two Bad Ants" is from TWO BAD ANTS by Chris Van Allsburg. Copyright © 1988 by Chris Van Allsburg. Reprinted by permission of Houghton Mifflin Company. All rights reserved.

"Who Has Seen the Wind?" by Christina Rossetti from THE RANDOM HOUSE BOOK OF POETRY FOR CHILDREN. Copyright © 1983 by Random House, Inc. Reprinted by permisssion of Random House, Inc.

Illustration

Mike DiGiorgio, 36; Leonor Glynn, 54; Leonor Glynn, 82; Mike DiGiorgio, 110; Jane Dill, 181; Pat Rasch, 280; Jane Dill, 332–333; Claude Martinot, 345; Lisa Desimini, 10–11; C. D. Hullinger, 122–123; Gail Piazza, 124–125; Mercedes McDonald, 248–249; Ray–Mel Cornelius, 250–251; Steve Adler, 356–357; John Carozza: 378; Rodica Prato: 377, 381, 385, 391.

Photography

5: (b.r.) Ken Bohn/Sea World San Diego. 7: (b.r.) Robert Eames/ Impact Visuals. 9: (b.r.) The Stock Market. 9: (t.r.) Tim Davis/Davis Lynn Images. 12: *Doubled Back* by Bev Doolittle (c) 1988, licensed by the Greenwich Workshop, Inc., Shelton, CT. 35: Francisco J. Rangel/The Image Works 38: National Gallery of Art, Washington, D.C., Chester Dale Collection. 40: Courtesy, Carmen Lomas Garza. 56: (c.) Carr Clifton. 58: (t.) Courtesy, Brenda Z. Guiberson. 58: (b.) Courtesy, Megan Lloyd. 80: James Blank/The Stock Market. 81: Rod Planck/Tony Stone Images. 84: The Bridgeman Art Library International. 86: b. Walker Books Limited/Photo courtesy of Candlewick Press. t. Walker Books Limited/Photo courtesy of Candlewick Press. 109: Michael Giannechini/Photo Researchers. 112-13: The Grand Design, Leeds, England/Superstock. 126: Courtesy of the Burke Museum of Natural History and Culture, catalog no. 2.5E1543, photo by Eduardo Calderón. 153: Courtesy, Ed Young. 156: PhotoDisc. 158: Photofest. 173: Courtesy, Seymour Simon. 178-79: Private Collection/Bridgeman Art Library. 180: Courtesy, Aliki. 206: Russian State Museum, St. Petersburg/AGE Fotostock/Superstock. 238-39: Christie's Images/Superstock. 244: Peter Arnold, Inc./ Kevin Schafer. 245: Stock Market/Bob London. 252: Christie's Images/The Bridgeman Art Library. 279: (t.r.) Benelux Press B.V./Photo Researchers, Inc. 282-83: Paul Ciesluk/Superstock. 284: Courtesy, Chris Van Allsburg. 312-313: Fine Art Photographic Library, London/Art Resource, NY. 314: Courtesy, Ellen Lambeth 314-15: Tim Davis/Davis/Lynn Images. 314: Davis/Lynn Images/Tim Davis. 317: Gail Shumway/FPG International. 318: Sorrel Wilby/Auscape International. 321: Gerry Ellis/ENP Images. 323: Kevin Horan Photography. 324: Flip Nicklin/Minden Pictures. 326: Gail Shumway/FPG International. 327: Tim Davis/Photo Researchers, Inc. 330: Butler Institute of American Art, Youngstown, OH/Bridgeman Art Library International/Superstock. 332: b.l. Photo courtesy of HarperCollins Publishers. 332: t.r. Photo courtesy of HarperCollins Publishers/Donald E. Johnson. 343: Renee Lynn/Tony Stone Images. 346: The Natural History Museum, London, UK. 352: (b.r.) Penny Tweedie/Tony Stone Images. 374 (l.) PhotoDisc. 376: Brownie Harris/The Stock Market. 380: Michal Heron/The Stock Market. 382: Arthur Beck /The Stock Market. 383: Gary Williams/Liaison International. 386: (b.l.) Frank Fournier/Contact Press/PNI. 389: Brian Stahlyk/Tony Stone Images. 392: Jon Feingersh/The Stock Market.

READING STRATEGY
Illustration

Krystyna Stasiak, pp. 13–13A; Mike DiGiorgio, pp. 113A, 179A, 239A, 347A; Diane Paterson, pp. 127–127A; Ron Himler, pp. 179–179A; Jared Lee, pp. 207–207A; David Galchutt, pp. 283–283A; Nicole Rutten, pp. 331–331A.

Photography

39-39a, Detroit Industry, North Wall, 1932-1933 by Diego Rivera. Gift of Edsel B. Ford. Photograph © 2001 The Detroit Institute of Arts; 39a (bottom), Corbis/Bettmann; 57-57a, Art Wolfe/Photo Researchers; 57, GC Kelley/Photo Researchers; 85-85a, Brandon D. Cole/Corbis; 85a (top), Gunter Marx/Corbis; 113 (top), Aaron Ferster/Photo Researchers; 113-113a (top), Superstock; 113-113a (bottom), Aaron Ferster/Photo Researchers; 159-159a, Art Wolfe/Stone; 239-239a, AP/Wide World Photos; 253-253a, Corbis/Bettmann; 313-313a, AP/Wide World Photos; 313a (top), Corbis/Bettmann; 347-347a, Superstock; 347a (inset), Alan Root/Photo Researchers.